GLYNDWR'S WAY

About the Authors

Ronnie and Chris, although originally from Plymouth and north Cornwall, have lived in north-east Wales for over 20 years. They have walked or climbed in many parts of the British Isles and completed several long-distance walks, including Offa's Dyke and the Cornish Coast Path. They felt it was time to get to know mid-Wales more intimately and decided on Glyndwr's Way. At the time there was not an adequate guidebook to Glyndwr's Way, so on their return they set about compiling one.

Chris has worked in outdoor education most of his working life, teaching a variety of sports and pursuits, including, of course, mountain walking skills. Chris undertook the majority of the route finding and planning, plus the photographs.

Ronnie works for Oswestry Borough Council and has written the guide and researched the background information to Glyndwr and the places visited.

GLYNDWR'S WAY

A WELSH NATIONAL TRAIL

by

Ronnie and Chris Catling

2 POLICE SQUARE, MILNTHORPE, CUMBRIA LA7 7PY
www.cicerone.co.uk

© Ronnie and Chris Catling 2005
ISBN 1 85284 299 7

A catalogue record for this book is available from the British Library.

OS Ordnance Survey® This product includes mapping data licensed from Ordnance Survey® with the permission of the Controller of Her Majesty's Stationery Office © Crown copyright 2002. *All rights reserved.*
Licence number PU100012932

Acknowledgements

Ronnie and Chris would like to thank Powys County Council for all their help including the publication of the many invaluable tourist guides to the various towns and villages visited en route, which have often been the starting point of more detailed research. Powys County Council also produces a set of sixteen guide leaflets to the route.

The Countryside Council for Wales must also be thanked for having the foresight to adopt Glyndwr's Way as the third National Trail in Wales.

Other people who have given their time are the curator of the Owain Glyndwr's Parliament House in Machynlleth and Mr Huw Jones of the Red Dragon.

Advice to Readers

Readers are advised that while every effort is taken by the authors to ensure the accuracy of this guidebook, changes can occur which may affect the contents. It is advisable to check locally on transport, accommodation, shops, etc, but even rights of way can be altered. Paths can be affected by forestry work, landslip or changes of ownership.

The authors would welcome information on any updates and changes sent through the publishers.

Front cover: View from the flanks of Foel Fadian

CONTENTS

Introduction..7
Owain Glyndwr 8
    The Welsh Revolt..8
    Legends, Myths and Traditions..17
Walking Glyndwr's Way..19
    Shopping, Public Transport and Accommodation 21
    Maps 22
Tourist Information Centres along the Route.....................................23
Itinerary...24

Section 1 Knighton to Felindre...26
Section 2 Felindre to Abbey-cwm-hir..35
Section 3 Abbey-cwm-hir to Llanidloes 44
Section 4 Llanidloes to Glaslyn..52
Section 5 Diversion – Glaslyn to Hyddgen 63
Section 6 Glaslyn to Machynlleth 66
Section 7 Machynlleth to Llanbrynmair..72
Section 8 Llanbrynmair to Llangadfan..80
Section 9 Llangadfan to Llanwddyn 85
Section 10 Llanwddyn to Pontrobert 90
Section 11 Pontrobert to Welshpool...97
Section 12 Welshpool to Knighton..107

Appendices
Appendix A: Bibliography 119
Appendix B: Summary of Route 120

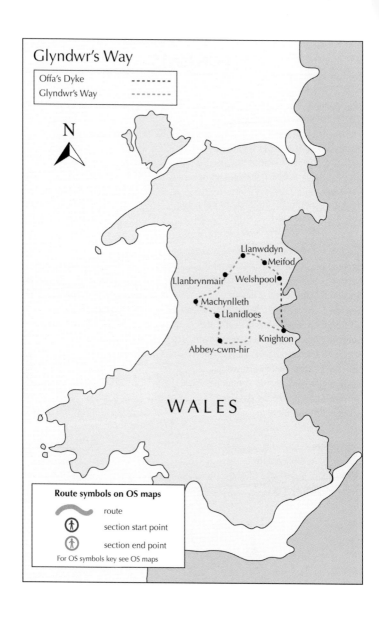

Glyndwr's Way

Offa's Dyke ‑‑‑‑‑‑‑‑
Glyndwr's Way ‑‑‑‑‑‑‑‑

N

Llanwddyn
Meifod
Llanbrynmair
Welshpool
Machynlleth
Llanidloes
Knighton
Abbey-cwm-hir

WALES

Route symbols on OS maps

route

section start point

section end point

For OS symbols key see OS maps

INTRODUCTION

Glyndwr's Way is named after Owain Glyndwr, who led the Welsh in a rebellion against the English in the 15th century. The Way was opened in 1977 as a recreational trail through Powys, and adopted as the third National Trail in Wales in 2000, celebrating the 600 years' anniversary of Glyndwr being declared Prince of Wales. The Way passes through farmland, forestry and open hill-land; it follows old Roman roads as well as drovers' roads and modern public rights of way. A link is made with Offa's Dyke at Welshpool, making a circular walk possible. The walk is full of interest with varied flora and fauna and geographical features. There are also many places of historical interest, many relating to Owain Glyndwr, which have legends and myths associated with them.

The area is sparsely populated even today which means walkers must be prepared to be independent of normal facilities such as shops and public transport on many of the sections.

Owain Glyndwr was descended from the royal lines of Powys and Deheubarth. He owned land at Glyndyfrdwy and Sycarth in the northeast of Wales, between the Tanat and Dee valleys. He turned what began as a border dispute with Lord Grey of Ruthin into a full-scale rebellion

Bugeilyn at the head of the Hengwm Valley (Section 5)

against Henry IV. Glyndwr was able to unite various rivalries amongst the Welsh and had many successes during the uprising by using guerrilla tactics and practising a scorched-earth policy. He was very nearly successful in achieving an independent and united Wales and his protest is the last sustained attempt made to achieve this through battle.

There are many myths, legends and stories told about Glyndwr, but it is certain that during the protest he and his supporters held on to this central part of Wales for most of the rebellion. The Welsh would have frequently crossed and recrossed mid-Wales during their many campaigns.

The opening chapter of the book gives a brief history of Owain Glyndwr and the Welsh Revolt together with a brief outline of the political and military events up to and during the rebellion. Details of a few prophecies, myths and legends and traditions surrounding Glyndwr are also included (for more detailed information refer to the Bibliography). The second chapter provides useful information on shopping, public transport and accommodation and a list of tourist information centres. The book then details 12 sections of the Way giving places of interest, facilities, such as shops, post offices and eating places, and directions, together with sketch maps. The route starts and finishes at Knighton; there is a diversion from the Way to take the walker out to Hyddgen to see the scene of a

decisive battle below the Plynlimon hills. From Welshpool a stretch of Offa's Dyke is taken to Knighton to complete the circuit.

OWAIN GLYNDWR

The Welsh Revolt

Little is known of Owain Glyndwr prior to him declaring himself Prince of Wales in September 1400. He was probably born at Sycarth, possibly at Glyndyfrdwy, both estates owned by his father, or maybe at the home of an aunt in south Wales, sometime in the 1350s – the exact year or date is not known. He was descended from the Princes of Powys and Deheubarth and could claim to be indirectly descended from the Princes of Gwynedd.

Glyndwr had both a military and a legal education as many minor squires' sons had at the time. Owain's father died at an early age and Sir David Hanmer was appointed his guardian. Owain spent several years at the Inns of Law in London and later followed a military career. Owain married Margaret, the daughter of his guardian. It seems that they lived a peaceful and idyllic life at Sycarth and produced nine children; six sons and three daughters.

For the period prior to declaring himself Prince of Wales, Glyndwr would be little remembered except for a famous legal battle in 1386 between Richard Lord Scrope and Sir Robert Grosvenor, in which he acted

Owain Glyndwr's standard (Section 2)

Owain Glyndwr's statue at Corwen

as a witness. He also supported Richard II in his battles with the Scots, the French and, possibly, the Irish. He does not appear to have distinguished himself sufficiently to be rewarded with a knighthood and eventually retired to his estates, a middle-aged country gentleman surrounded by his family. But his life was soon to change.

There was already a general feeling of unrest amongst the Welsh prior to 1400. The English aristocracy were taxing the Welsh very heavily with many thousands of pounds pouring from Wales into English coffers. Richard II's mysterious disappearance aggravated the situation. The Welsh people were as loyal to him as

they had been to his father, the Black Prince. Many Englishmen were given high appointments throughout Wales, overlooking native candidates for bishoprics or stewardships. Glyndwr's own failure to be knighted after serving his king is one example of Welsh services going unrewarded. Hopcyn ap Tomas, a scribe of the time, described the Welsh as 'suffering pain and deprivation and exile ... of such resentments are the ingredients of revolt assembled'.

The oppression of the Welsh people may have continued if quarrels had not arisen between Owain Glyndwr and his neighbour at Glyndyfrdwy, the English Lord Grey of Ruthin. Two reasons are given for this

9

The Hyddgen Stones are visited in Section 5

dispute, either or both may be true. The first reason was a simple boundary dispute between the two landowners in which Parliament and, more importantly, Henry IV refused to support a Welshman against an English lord. The second reason given is that Lord Grey was commissioned to deliver a summons to Glyndwr requiring him to join the proposed royal expedition to Scotland. Grey delayed the delivery of the message for several days, leaving it too late for Glyndwr to be able to accept the invitation. Reginald Grey reported back to Henry IV in a detrimental manner. This appears to have been the turning point for Owain.

Whatever the particular reason, or reasons, that sparked off Glyndwr taking action, it seems he was destined to lead the Welsh people. The Welsh paid great attention to their ancestors and Glyndwr's were impeccable, descended as he was from the Welsh princes; besides, the bards had been preparing Glyndwr for this eventuality. He satisfied many of the traditions handed down from Merlin and Taliesin of a Welsh saviour in time of need and that time seemed to have come.

Glyndwr met with a small band of supporters, which included his eldest son, his brothers-in-law, and the dean of St Asaph at Glyndyfrdwy on 16 September 1400 and declared himself Prince of Wales. This marked the start of the rebellion. Throughout the rebellion this declaration never seems to have been questioned. At no time was there a struggle for leadership, although many areas appear to have conducted affairs on their own behalf under the banner of Glyndwr. Two days after the declaration a small army attacked Ruthin Castle and various English castles and estates in the north-east of Wales were assaulted over the next five days. From then onwards the revolt escalated, with Owain Glyndwr as its leader. It was the signal for all Welshmen to flock together.

Most of the action was of a hit-and-run, guerrilla type, taking place in many parts of Wales, led by many different local supporters. In 1401 Glyndwr and his men hid out in the mountains of Wales. There were various localised skirmishes throughout the country, including the taking of Conway Castle. The most important battle of the year took place at Hyddgen. This site, on the slopes of Plynlimon, is where Glyndwr had a large camp in the early years of the rebellion, now under the Nant-y-moch Reservoir. Glyndwr and his men were attacked here by Flemings, whose forebears had been brought to south Wales by Henry I to work in the woollen craft industry. Owain and his men were caught by surprise by an army three times their number. The Flemings' onslaught was, however, defeated and they took flight. This event inspired large numbers of Welshmen from all over Wales and, also, those living and working in England, to join in the rebellion. Years later two white stones were placed in the valley to honour this first real battle and major success.

In 1402 the Welshmen again attacked and this time took Ruthin Castle, taking Reginald Grey prisoner. A ransom was demanded and paid, leaving Earl Grey to spend the rest of his life in poverty. This success was

Bryn Glas, passed in Section 6

the impetus required and the rebels entered Gwent and Glamorgan and threatened Usk, Newport and Cardiff. A battle at Pilleth was a momentous moment in the revolt. Owain and his men overwhelmed an English army on a hill at Bryn Glas, close to the English border, proving that the Welsh were a force to be reckoned with. Edmund Mortimer, who was the uncle to the 10 year-old Earl of March, was captured at Pilleth. A ransom demanded for his release was not paid by Henry IV as the Earl of March was the direct lineal heir to the crown. (Henry IV had seized the throne from Richard II. The Earl of March was Richard II's named heir so Henry thought his position would be safer if Edmund Mortimer was kept a prisoner by Glyndwr, especially as the Welsh people had been supporters of Richard II.) Mortimer joined the rebel cause and married Catherine (one of Glyndwr's daughters) later in the year, a diplomatic success likened to the military success of Pilleth. It is thought that Glyndwr used Mortimer to try to negotiate a settlement with the English at this time. However, these negotiations were unsuccessful.

There does not seem to have been a deliberate plan to the attacks, although a scorched-earth policy was practised by both the Welsh and the English. Both sides thought that by either using all the crops and food available in an area or destroying what could not be carried away,

they would weaken the enemy. Throughout the revolt Glyndwr and his armies were able to travel freely across Wales, appearing and disappearing at ease.

During 1402 Henry IV sent three armies into Wales, led respectively by himself, the English Prince of Wales and the Earl of Stafford, in an attempt to curb the rebellion. Glyndwr and his men evaded these armies while the atrocious weather drove the English back across the border after only three weeks.

Glyndwr now negotiated support from the Percys, a discontented Northumbrian family. In July 1403 the Percys, headed by Henry Hotspur, joined the revolt at Chester. The King, on his way to Scotland, was unaware of this. When he found out, he made a hurried journey to meet Hotspur a few miles from Shrewsbury. Glyndwr with his '8000 lancers' was delayed by successful actions in south and west Wales and was unable to support Hotspur in time. Hotspur's father and his men, who were due to join Hotspur, had not yet left Northumberland. Hotspur was slain in battle and his men defeated. Had this battle been successful Welsh history would have been different.

However, the Welsh rebels continued with their guerrilla tactics throughout Wales from the north to the Bristol Channel. During August and September Glyndwr was said to have invaded Shropshire, Chester and as far north as the Wirral and skirmishes were reported all along the border between Wales and England.

In September the King again headed an expedition into Wales. The campaign was short lived, partly because of the difficulties of supplying a large army with food and equipment. He retreated to Hereford in October having encountered little opposition. During the last three months of 1403, Glyndwr and his armies were engaged in events throughout Wales and were now receiving help from the French.

By 1404 the revolt was gathering pace and was not going to be the nine-day wonder Henry IV had thought it would be. Glyndwr took both Harlech and Aberystwyth castles in the spring of the year, installing his family at Harlech, which gave him a base and complete control of central Wales. He turned to statesmanship, declaring a parliament at Machynlleth, which was in the centre of the area that was under his absolute control. Tradition says that Owain Glyndwr was crowned Prince of Wales at this parliament with emissaries from Scotland, France and Spain attending. In May John Hanmer, Owain Glyndwr's brother-in-law, and Gruffydd Young, his chancellor, went to France to negotiate with Charles VI. Glyndwr sent a letter (the Pennal Letter) to the French king requesting help and, for the first time in writing, used the title 'Prince of Wales'. A document was signed in July uniting France and Wales against 'Henry of Lancaster' (Henry IV).

Successful attacks continued in south Wales throughout the summer. Archenfield, Abergavenny, Craig-y-Dorth, Monmouth and Glamorgan all succumbed to the Welsh – although the Welsh were defeated by the Earl of Warwick at Campstone. In July a French fleet was reported cruising in the Bristol Channel, but the French never landed.

The year 1404 was one in which Glyndwr strengthened his position. He now had to gain and maintain his hold over all of Wales, not just the central region.

Owain Glyndwr continued to have small successes during 1405, but so did the English Prince of Wales, to whom Henry IV had given sole responsibility for the Welsh problem early in 1404. In February 1405 Glyndwr, Lord Percy and Edmund Mortimer agreed on an alliance, which they named the Tripartite Indenture. The Tripartite Indenture divided England in two – a part each for Percy and Mortimer – and slightly extended the border of Wales into England for Glyndwr and the Welsh; it was never the intention of the Welsh rebels to claim the throne of England. Glyndwr then, later in the year, held a second parliament, at Harlech. He also invited both the French and the Irish to help him free Wales for the Welsh.

The first Welsh defeat of the year occurred at Grosmont. This was followed by a major loss in May at Usk when Glyndwr's brother, Tudur,

The front of Parliament
House, Machynlleth
(Section 6)

was 'put to the sword in front of the castle'. Glyndwr's eldest son, Gruffydd, was also captured. He was sent to the Tower of London and after six years died in prison. Henry IV planned another foray into Wales and successfully retook Beaumaris Castle on Anglesey.

The French now joined the fray, landing at Milford Haven, and, together with Glyndwr's men, an army said to number 10,000 attacked Haverford West, Tenby, Carmarthen and Cardigan before heading west into Herefordshire and Worcestershire, where Henry's men met the combined forces of the Welsh and the French. There was no decisive battle, each side had minor skirmishes until Glyndwr had to retire into Wales as he was unable to obtain supplies for his men. Never again were the Welsh given a similar chance to defeat the English. It was the beginning of the end of Welsh hopes for an independent and free Wales. However, all was not yet over. Many of the French force stayed on to face the winter in Wales. Gloucester and Hereford supported the Welsh with supplies, while Pembroke offered a truce.

In the late winter of 1406 the French left the country. Scotland too had its own problems and the English defeated the Welsh in a battle on St George's Day. The Gower and Anglesey abandoned the rebellion and submitted to the English. Throughout the year, however, Glyndwr was able to maintain his position in central Wales with Harlech and Aberystwyth castles under his control. There was little change on either side, although Prince Henry made a bold attempt to recapture Aberystwyth Castle, but underestimated Glyndwr's determination.

During 1407 events in France produced a truce between the English and the French from which the Welsh were excluded. Glyndwr could not count on the French for any further support. The rebellion was wavering and Glyndwr was finding it difficult to find troops. It became increasingly impossible to maintain the ground he had gained.

Harlech and Aberystwyth castles fell to the English. The loss of Harlech Castle was a heavy blow to Owain as his wife, two daughters and three of Edmund Mortimer's children were captured and taken to London. Mortimer himself died during the siege, together with many other loyal supporters. Glyndwr had now lost control of a large part of western Wales and he could no longer maintain his role as the ruling prince. He was once again a guerrilla leader. However, Glyndwr himself eluded capture and, with his only surviving son, Maredudd, disappeared into central Wales. The Welsh did not make any great attacks throughout the next two years, merely harrying the English as and when they could.

In 1408 and 1409 events in the north of England and elsewhere left Glyndwr with still fewer allies. The

View of Welshpool from Long Mountain, Section 12

rebellion was gradually dying away. The rebels still had control of large parts of central and north-eastern Wales and in 1412 Glyndwr made a huge effort to turn events to his advantage once again by heading an attack into Shropshire. However, he and his army did not get any further than Welshpool, where three of his strongest supporters were taken prisoner. He did not give up hope as much of central Wales was loyal to the cause. However, as time went on, little was heard of the rebels apart from minor skirmishes and successes. By 1413 no one knew where Glyndwr was and he was heard of no more. Prince Henry became Henry V early that year and offered a pardon to Owain Glyndwr, which was never accepted. The offer was made again and again to both

Glyndwr and his supporters through Glyndwr's son, Maredudd. However, even as late as 1415 Glyndwr's supporters continued to try to negotiate help from the French.

Glyndwr's legacy remains; J.E. Lloyd wrote in his *Owain Glyndwr* that Glyndwr's '...courage and high spirit have never been impugned and it is clear testimony to the loyalty and affection which he inspired that not even in his darkest hour was anyone found to betray him to his foes ... For the Welshmen of all subsequent ages, Glyndwr has been a national hero, the first, indeed, in the country's history to command the willing support alike of north and south, east and west, Gwynedd and Powys, Deheubarth and Morgannwg.'

When Henry Tudor won the battle of Bosworth on 22 August 1485 the

Venetian Ambassador to the English remarked 'The Welsh may now be said to have recovered their former independence, for the most wise and fortunate Henry VII is a Welshman.'

Legends, myths and traditions

Shakespeare immortalised Owain Glyndwr and referred to the mysteries surrounding his life with these lines:

'These signs have mark'd me extraordinary; And all the courses of my life do show I am not in the roll of common men.' *Henry IV Part I*

Owain Glyndwr is associated with many myths, legends and traditions concerning his life and his role as a leader of the Welsh people. The circumstances of Glyndwr's birth and tales from his childhood up until the uprising were interpreted by the prophets, who spread the word that a Welsh hero had risen to fight for Welsh freedom.

Much of the mystery surrounding Glyndwr is due to the clever tricks he employed to fool his enemies and to the bardic poets and storytellers who developed and spread the tales told about him.

It is told that, when Glyndwr was born, the stables of his father's horses ran fetlock deep in blood. As Owain grew from babyhood to boyhood he would scream every time he saw a bow and arrow or spear and would only stop when he was allowed to touch the weapon. These stories, and others like them, prophesied his ability to be a soldier.

Iolo Goch and Gruffyd Llwyd, Welsh bardic poets, both composed poems in honour of Glyndwr. The poems concerned his life before 16 September 1400. Iolo Goch composed three poems. The first describes Glyndwr's lineage, a common form of tribute to a person descended from the various Princes of Wales. The second describes Glyndwr's successes and heroic feats in Scotland. The third describes his peaceful and comfortable house at Sycarth, which was built by the Normans and is featured in the *Domesday Book*, the only stronghold in the locality to do so. Gruffyd Llwyd also describes Glyndwr's exploits in Scotland and, in a second poem, gently hints that Owain Glyndwr will lead the Welsh to an independent Wales, thus fulfilling an age-old prophesy. Glyndwr himself believed in these prophecies and almost certainly had his own personal prophet who interpreted various portents and signs for him and who also advised him on various other matters.

Legend has it that when Glyndwr was proclaimed Prince of Wales on 16 September 1400 four bells at the four corners of a shrine in Westminster rang of their own accord, not once but four times. At the same time the stream at Cilmery, in which the severed head of Llywelyn the Last had been washed, ran red with blood.

When a comet crossed the sky in February 1402 the bards declared there had been such a sign at the birth of Arthur and there had also been a

17

large star over Bethlehem. When viewed from England the comet pointed towards Wales and occasionally it curled its tail or took on the shape of a dragon. These sightings coincided with horrendous thunderstorms and Glyndwr captured his greatest enemy, Reginald Grey. Not only did the comet portray success for the Welsh but the adverse weather added to Glyndwr's mystique in that he was able to call down the weather to help them gain that success! This established Glyndwr's reputation. He was the warrior king. He was Celtic freedom reborn, prophesied by Merlin and bards from ancient times.

Glyndwr's personal prophet warned him about his cousin Hywel Sele, who did not agree with the rebellion and did not support Glyndwr. So, during a visit to Hywel's estate, Glyndwr wore chain mail under his ordinary clothes. The two cousins went out hunting together and Hywel raised his bow and arrow to, supposedly, shoot at deer, but instead fired at his cousin. Glyndwr was, of course, unharmed thanks to the warning he had received, but Hywel Sele was never seen again … or was he? Some 40 years later an oak tree on Hywel Sele's estate was struck by lightning and split open. Revealed inside the great tree was the skeleton of a man …

Owain was also advised that he would be captured somewhere between Carmarthen and Gower. So he avoided the area, unlike his ally,

Henry Hotspur, who had been warned that he would meet his death at Berwick. Little knowing that the name was not only that of a town near the Scottish Border, but also a little, unknown hamlet near Shrewsbury, he went to the latter, where he met his death in battle with the King.

As the rebellion gathered pace so did the tales of Glyndwr's mystical powers. Twice during the rebellion the English had to turn back because of the dreadful weather apparently called down by Glyndwr to thwart them in their endeavours. The tales of his disappearances when surrounded by the King's men were also many and varied. These magical disappearances were actually due to Glyndwr's wily tricks and clever subterfuge, but they contributed to his reputation. Time after time he showed how he could ride across Wales, suddenly appearing out of the mountains or mists like a demon to take the English by surprise. He was able to disappear again as easily; a servant would dress in his clothes, or his servants were ordered to pretend that he was dead so that he could make his escape. There are many caves throughout Wales that are named after him, in which, no doubt, he used to hide out.

On one occasion he ordered all the horses' shoes to be put on backwards to confuse the enemy while he and his men made their escape. Several stories tell of the Welsh dressing scarecrows, putting them out where they could be seen to mislead the English into thinking the Welsh were lying in wait for them. The story-tellers made much of these escapes and explained they were all possible because a raven had given Glyndwr a stone that made him invisible.

Other tales are told of his incredible strength. He is said to have gouged marks in stones where his sword landed after he had tossed it in the air in joy after a victory or when he had thrown it in impatience, as at Corwen. He is also said to have left the marks of his knees in stone where he had knelt. Even his horse is said to have left the imprints of his hooves in stone! Further testament to his strength is a climb in north Wales, which, according to climbers' guides, Glyndwr was the first person to climb during one of his many escapes.

Is it any wonder then that the end of his life should be a mystery? Some say he retired to live with his daughter at Monnington in Herefordshire, but there are many tales throughout Wales of the cave where he still sleeps with his men until the Welsh need him again.

So the man who came from nowhere returned to nowhere. There is no grave, no headstone, no memorial to the man who tried to free Wales 'one hundred years too early', in the words of the Abbot of Vale Crucis Abbey. The poets composed no epitaph for him; after all he is not dead.

WALKING GLYNDWR'S WAY

Glyndwr's Way was established in the 1970s by Powys County Council, who manage the route with the assistance of the Countryside Council for Wales. In 1993 a project officer was employed by the County Council to develop the route to the standard of a National Trail. This was achieved and the Welsh Assembly granted the Way National Trail status in the autumn of 2000, within weeks of the anniversary of the uprising of Glyndwr on 16 September 1400. Landowners, contractors and volunteers have helped to carry out improvement works and maintenance of the path.

Originally the intention was to officially launch Glyndwr's Way as a National Trail in spring 2001 but the foot and mouth disaster of that year postponed the event until April 2002. There were simultaneous ceremonies at Knighton, Welshpool and Machynlleth on 19 April when the Lord Lieutenant of Powys, the Hon. Mrs S. Legge-Burke, unveiled a plinth

Glyndwr's Way sign

in Knighton High Street, and Sue Essex AM (Assembly Minister for the Environment) and Iolo Williams (Welsh broadcaster) unveiled similar plinths in Machynlleth and Welshpool.

There are also four sections of the path that have not yet been brought up to National Trail standards, the alternatives to these sections are described. To make this a circular walk there is an added section from Welshpool to Knighton along the Offa's Dyke National Trail.

The walk takes you from a small market town on the border of Wales and England around the central massif of mid-Wales, across bogs, rivers and streams, following Roman roads, old green roads, drovers' roads, public footpaths, bridleways and country lanes. You will experience a diversity of landscape from gentle rolling farmland to upland sheep-grazing hills; from open moorland to heavily forested valleys; massive conifer plantations to mixed deciduous woodland; remote farming communities and hidden valleys to villages and towns.

The flora and fauna are as varied as the scenery, with each day's walking bringing new surprises. The area sustains a rich and varied bird life – consider yourself very unlucky if you don't see at least one red kite. The history of the area is as diverse as the geography. The area is largely unspoilt, peaceful and far from the maddening crowd.

There are a number of areas and sites of historical interest along the Way that will add to your enjoyment of the walk.

You can expect a variety of different weather conditions regardless of the time of year because the prevailing winds sweep in across the Irish Sea. So, be well prepared. Walking boots must be worn on some of the routes described.

It is recommended that the whole route is completed in order to obtain the maximum enjoyment from the walk. However, it is feasible to walk the route in stages.

You may be tempted to omit the route out to Abbey-cwm-hir and back

Welsh poppies

Kingcups

to Bwlch-y-sarnau, but you will miss breathtaking views over some of the most remote parts of Wales, the opportunity of possibly seeing red kites, the peace and tranquillity of Abbey-cwm-hir itself, and the hospitality of the local inn; in exchange you will gain several miles of road plodding with very little of interest along the route. You may also be sorely tempted not to walk out to Hyddgen, especially if you are camping. But this may be the most exciting route of the whole walk for you! Initially there is little of note: a wide flat valley walk in which the River Hengwm meanders on its way to join the Hyddgen before adding its water to the Nant-y-moch Reservoir. The floor of the valley is wet and covered in reeds and tough mountain grasses. However, eventually your goal is reached: two vaguely discernible white boulders, nearly lost beneath the mountain grass. These boulders are a reminder that once this valley was alive with the clash of swords, the whoosh of flying arrows and the cries of men and horses in a battle that changed the history of Wales.

Again you may be tempted to go directly from Llangadfan to Llwydiarth thus omitting the Vyrnwy Reservoir and Llanwddyn Village; after all you have already visited the Clywedog. However, you will miss the fairy tale setting of the valley and its pumping house. It is a fairly easy day's walk and refreshments are normally available at the dam end of Vyrnwy.

Observe the country code. Leave all gates as you find them. If you absolutely have to climb a gate, do so at the hinges, where it is strongest. Leave nothing but footprints and take nothing but photos. If you are walking with a dog please keep it under control at all times; farmers welcome well-behaved, well-trained dogs more than they do the owners! Quite rightly, however, they can be very irritated by badly-behaved dogs. If in sheep country keep the dog on a lead when requested to do so, or at least keep the lead in a handy pocket. If in cattle country and the cattle stampede, let the dog go – it will run faster than you or the cattle!

Shopping, public transport and accommodation

Mid-Wales is not a highly populated area. Most communities are widely spread and there are very few shops. The main shopping centres are Knighton, Llanidloes, Machynlleth and Welshpool. You really do need to be completely self-sufficient between the four main towns, especially if you are camping. There are no banks outside these towns. Many small villages do have post offices, but, beware; some do not open every day of the week or are only open at certain times of the day. These village post offices may also sell a limited number of groceries, newspapers and films but very little else.

Information on accommodation and public transport will enable you

Section 6 passes Foel Fadian with Glaslyn in the foreground

to plan the length of each day's walk. The routes in the book are not intended to be adhered to absolutely, so plan each day's walking to suit your capability. Accommodation and transport information can be obtained by post in advance.

The *Wales, Bus, Rail and Tourist Map and Guide* is available through the tourist information centres (listed below). This is a public transport map for the whole of Wales. For more detailed information request the *Travel Guide*. The tourist information centre at Knighton will send you train timetables, the *Powys Bus Timetable* and a list of accommodation available throughout the length of the walk, which will be useful to you. The accommodation listed is approved by the Welsh Tourist Board as achieving certain standards. There are other places to stay, but the information on

these can only be obtained locally; this can be found on local tourist information boards, normally located outside village post offices, or centrally in the village. Another useful publication is the *Montgomeryshire Information Brochure*, published every year, available from Welshpool Tourist Information Centre. This covers nearly the whole route and gives information on local bird life, flora and fauna, places of interest and lists of accommodation.

Maps

The Ordnance Survey maps which cover the area are the Landranger Series numbers 125, 126, 135, 136, 137 and 148.

The maps used to show the route in this guide are taken from the Landranger series and are at a scale of 1:50,000.

Knighton Tourist Information Centre
Offa's Dyke Centre
West Street
Knighton LD7 1EW
Tel. 01547 529424

This is the main centre for Glyndwr's Way, as well as Offa's Dyke National Trail, where you can obtain a leaflet giving Welsh Tourist Board approved bed and breakfast establishments, hotels and campsites. For other accommodation that is not approved by the Tourist Board enquire locally.

Llanidloes Tourist Information Centre
54 Long Bridge Street
Llanidloes SY18 6EF
Tel. 01686 412605

Machynlleth Tourist Information Centre
Canolfan Owain Glyndwr
Machynlleth SY20 8EE
Tel. 01654 702401

This is open all year round during the week. It is next door to Glyndwr's Parliament House.

Lake Vyrnwy Tourist Information Centre
Unit 2, Vyrnwy Craft Workshops
Lake Vyrnwy SY10 0LY
Tel. 01691 870346

Welshpool Tourist Information Centre
Vicarage Garden
Church Street
Welshpool SY21 7DD
Tel. 01938 552043
Tel. 01938 552043

ITINERARY
(note all distances are approximate)

Section	Places passed	Distance	Map
Section 1	Knighton – Garth Hill – Llangunllo – Beacon Common – Warren Brook – Cefn Pawl – Felindre	25km (15½ miles)	OS 136/137
Section 2	Felindre – Rhuvid – Castell-y-blaidd – Llanbadarn Fynydd – Moel Dod – Tynypant – Abbey-cwm-hir	25km (15½ miles)	OS 136
Section 3	Abbey-cwm-hir – Bwlch-y-sarnau – Bailey Bog – Prysgduon – Newchapel – Llanidloes	24.5km (15¼ miles)	OS 136
Section 4	Llanidloes – Allt Goch – Bryn-Tail – Llyn Clywedog – Hafren Forest – Clywedog Gorge – Glaslyn	24km (15 miles)	OS 136
Section 5	Glaslyn – Bugeilyn – Hyddgen – Bugeilyn – Glaslyn	17km (10½ miles)	OS 135
Section 6	Glaslyn – Foel Fadian – Nantyfyda – Cleiriau-isaf – Talbontdrain – Bryn Glas – Machynlleth	20km (12½ miles)	OS 135
Section 7	Machynlleth – Forge – Penegoes – Abercegir – Cefn Coch – Cemmaes Road – Commins Gwalia – Gwern y Bwlch – Llanbrynmair	25km (15½ miles)	OS 135/125
Section 8	Llanbrynmair – Bryn Gwyn – Nant-yr-Eira – Dolwen – Pen Coed – Llangadfan	17.5km (11 miles)	OS 136/125
Section 9	Llangadfan – Dyfnant Forest – Ddol Cownwy – Llanwddyn	12km (7½ miles)	OS 125

Section	Places passed	Distance	Map
Section 10	Llanwddyn – Llwydiarth (Pont Llogel) – Dolwar Fach – Allt Dolanog – Dolanog – Doladron – Pontrobert	18km (11¼ miles)	OS 125
Section 11	Pontrobert – Gallt yr Ancr – Meifod – Broniarth Hill – Llyn Du – Figyn Wood – Y Golfa – Welshpool	22.5km (14 miles)	OS 125/126
Section 12	Welshpool – Long Mountain – Forden – Mellington – Churchtown – Bryndrinog – Spoad Hill – Llanfair Hill – Panpunton – Knighton	47km (29¼ miles)	OS 126/137
	Total distance:	**277.5km (172½ miles)**	

SECTION 1

Knighton to Felindre

25km (15½ miles)

Maps required:	OS Landranger 136/137
Height gain:	600m

This section offers a gentle introduction to the whole route and includes most of the different types of scenery to be found throughout Glyndwr's Way. Parts of this section are exposed especially on Beacon Common. Total height climbed is approximately 600m with a height of approximately 500m being reached on the flanks of Stanky Hill.

You leave Knighton by walking up the steep Narrows, possibly the hardest bit of the route! The Way follows the back streets of Knighton, dropping down to a stream before climbing uphill again and delving into Garth Wood, a mixed deciduous wood with a high canopy. Thereafter there are country lanes, green lanes and farm tracks through fields to Llangunllo, a distance of about 10km or 6 miles.

Llangunllo has a village community shop and a public house. An overnight stay can be made here if necessary.

After leaving Llangunllo by road the route enters fields and eventually a green lane which follows an exposed ridge, giving good views. It is then uphill to Beacon Common and open heather moorland. Rough, open pastureland comes after Warren Brook before dropping down through fields to Felindre.

The facilities at Felindre include a post office and village store and there are limited camping facilities.

To navigate out of **Knighton**, from the Clock Tower go straight up High Street (The Narrows), turn left and bear right and then turn left again to go down a footpath. Come out onto a lane and go straight across, downhill to a stream. Follow the footpath until it joins a lane, turn left

KNIGHTON

Knighton is a pleasant country town situated on the banks of the River Teme and the border between Wales and England, the only town of any size to do so. Tref-y-Clawdd, the Welsh name for the town, means 'Town on the Dyke', the dyke being that built by King Offa in the eighth century.

The Offa's Dyke National Trail passes through the town and there are many fine stretches of Offa's Dyke to the north and south of the town, as well as in Knighton itself. Knighton is home to the Offa's Dyke Centre, which is also the local tourist information centre. It is situated beside a park that has a commemorative pillar to the opening of the trail in 1971.

The English translation 'Knight's Town' or 'Town of the Horsemen' refers to the town's strategic position in the defences of the Welsh Marches. The town boasts the sites of two motte and bailey castles: the Normans built the first wooden structure, Bryn-y-Castell, close to the banks of the Teme in about 1100 – the mound and ditch of Bryn-y-Castell can still be seen behind the cricket ground. Later the Normans decided a better defensive position would be on top of the hill so another was built on the hill overlooking the Teme.

The Normans built many wooden motte and bailey castles throughout Wales and many had the wooden tower rebuilt in stone. The tower or castle, whether of wood or stone, was built on a man-made mound, the motte. The building was often no more than a fortified house, normally surrounded by at least a ditch but sometimes by a moat. The bailey was outside this and possibly contained the baron's or knight's living quarters, although, more often than not, the baron lived on the motte and the servants were quartered in the bailey, which housed the kitchens, stables and barns. The bailey was surrounded by a wooden fence or palisade. The daily business of the servants was carried out in the bailey with people and animals resorting to the castle only in time of danger.

The castle at the top of the town was rebuilt of stone when the Mortimers governed the town. The older part of the town was built around the remains of this castle, with more modern buildings flowing downhill. The Clock Tower was donated by Thomas Moreton in 1872 and is the official start of Glyndwr's Way. A few yards up the pedestrianised street, known locally as The Narrows, is a stone plinth unveiled by the Lord Lieutenant of Powys, the Hon. Mrs S. Legge-Burke, on 19 April 2002 when Glyndwr's Way was opened as Wales's third national trail.

St Edmund's Church is built on the north side of the town and, apart from the medieval tower, dates from 1876. When the bells are rung, they echo along the valley of the River Teme.

Employment today is supplied by small industry, agriculture (it is a market town) and tourism. There are a wide variety of shops, a post office, banks, hotels and public houses as well as camping facilities.

onto the lane and almost immediately right, up a right of way, cross a cul-de-sac and continue on the right of way to a main road. Cross the road. Set back and slightly to the left is a waymark that indicates a footpath up beside some houses. At the top of this path is Garth Lane, turn right onto the lane and almost immediately left to follow a footpath in front of cottages and on to a green lane.

Knighton is below to the right. Follow the fence on the right, go over the stile and bear left onto a second path and almost immediately right into a deciduous wood, contouring around Garth Hill – the B4355 Knighton to Newtown road is below through the trees. The path curves away left as it comes out of the woods and becomes a green lane. When the green lane joins a minor road turn left and uphill, at a Y-junction turn left,

Map continues p.30

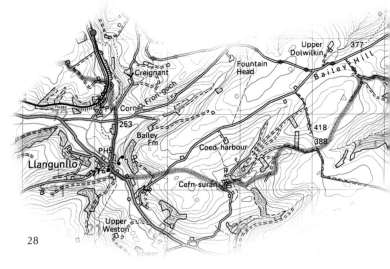

go straight ahead and downhill at the next junction. At the bottom of the hill turn right to go uphill.

Follow the waymark signs up the slopes of Bailey Hill, through the fields, first keeping the hedge on the right and then after a stream, on the left to a cross-roads in the tracks, turn left.

Follow this track through the fields turning left off the track into a field just after a conifer plantation. Go diagonally right downhill and cross a stream, about halfway up the track turn right and go downhill to a gate. Go through and follow the edge of this field, through a gate, turn right onto a track, turn left at the next junction to go through a farm, going over a cattle grid and across a garden, climb through a gap in the hedge and over a stile, turn left onto a track. Turn almost

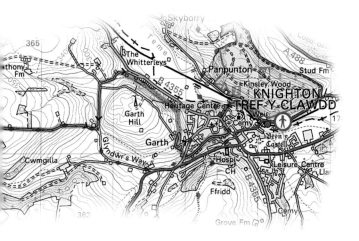

Garth Wood

immediately right, follow the track through one field and over a stile. Bear slightly right to a stile, climb over and turn slightly right again to another stile, go over this turning left onto a road.

Almost immediately and on a slight bend go over a stile on the right. Descend through

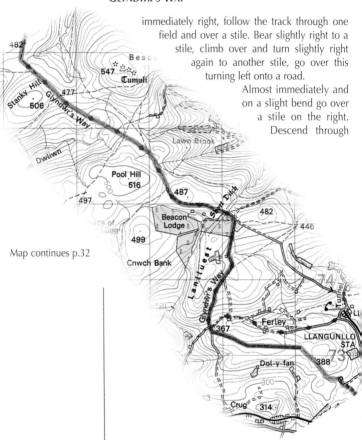

Map continues p.32

two fields to a farm track, cross this and bear right to a corner of the field. Enter a green lane that leads to the B4356, turn right to the village of **Llangunllo**.

Turn right at the crossroads in the middle of the village and go straight across at the next crossroads. On a right-hand bend turn left through a waymarked gate, across a field and down to a stream. Cross the stream by a bridge, through three fields following a hedge on the

LLANGUNLLO

Llangunllo is a quiet village, built by the River Lugg, some 2.5km (1½ miles) from the railway station with the same name. The village has a community run village shop and public house. The church is dedicated to the Celtic Saint Cynllo. There was a village school here as early as 1650 which finally closed in 1984.

Llangunllo Church

Beacon Common is Crown Estates land and is managed by them and Radnorshire Wildlife Trust.

left. Go through a gate onto a road and keep straight ahead to go under the Heart of Wales railway at Pye Corner, turn immediately left after the railway bridge over a cattle grid to go up a farm track. Follow the track around the edge of the fields. After 750m the route turns left off the track through a gate on the left just before a gate and farm buildings. Contour around to the right of a hill to a gate in a corner of a field, go through and immediately left through another gate. Go right over the shoulder of a hill in this field to a gate in a corner, go straight across two fields and turn left into a green lane. Continue along the ridge to a crossroads, turn right and follow a track uphill to Beacon Common and **Short Ditch**. Beacon Common is crisscrossed with tracks and is fairly featureless; great care must be taken with navigation. ◄

From the conifer plantation just before Short Ditch, turn left and follow the waymark, stay on the main track; contour around Pool Hill in a northerly direction. Four tracks meet almost together at GR180757 where the ground is very broken by vehicle tracks and can be wet. Keep to the left junction at both junctions and continue to contour around Pool Hill in a north-westerly direction. Drop down slightly before going up over the shoulder of Stanky Hill, Beacon Hill is on the right. Contour around Stanky Hill until

SHORT DITCH

Short Ditch is a heather covered rampart some 300m long and is said to be the remains of a forward defence constructed by Edmund Mortimer to protect Knighton from Owain Glyndwr. If this is so, Mortimer's attempts were unsuccessful because Glyndwr destroyed the castle in Knighton in 1402. Other theories link this ditch and others in the area to the building of Offa's Dyke, or part of piecemeal defences built either before or after Offa's Dyke.

GR164767, where there is a very marshy piece of ground and, again, the track is very broken up. Just after this, as the main track turns to the left, there is an indistinct track to the right. Turn off the main track here to contour over Black Mountain. Stanky Hill will now be behind.

Short Ditch,
Beacon Common

Follow the not very distinct track over the side of Black Mountain and drop down to some trees and Warren Brook. Cross the brook and turn right, follow the obvious path in a northerly direction, keeping to the high ground for about 1km (½ mile) before dropping down to a track and following the waymarks.

At Cefn Pawl, a farmstead, cross the field diagonally left to a corner of a fence and follow the fence to a track. Bear right and go through a gate, turning left off the track at a waymark. Lapwings can be both seen and heard on this open moorland. Cross this field staying parallel with some trees to the right. There is a waymark halfway along the field. Continue contouring until the fence on the right drops down to a wood. Follow this fence to the corner, go through a gate on the right, cross the next field to another gate and stile. Climb this stile and follow the track down to Brandy House Farm, turn left to a road, the B4355. Turn left again into **Felindre**.

FELINDRE

Felindre is a small village on the B4355 in the valley of the River Teme. There is a post office with a general store.

SECTION 2

Felindre to Abbey-cwm-hir

25km (15½ miles)

Maps required:	OS Landranger 136
Height gain:	520m

This section travels mostly through exposed moorland or upland pasturage and is more strenuous than the first section but only climbs to a total height of approximately 520m, the highest point being the trig point on Ysgwd-ffordd at about 470m.

The route starts on farmland then, after passing several trout ponds, crosses open moorland and upland pastures to Castell-y-blaidd. There are many fine views along the Gwenlas Brook Valley and across mid-Wales before the route descends to Llanbadarn Fynydd, a village on the A483. This is a distance of about 12km or 7½ miles.

Llanbadarn Fynydd has a village community shop with refreshments, a petrol station and a post office. There is also a public house offering accommodation.

After leaving the village, past the church, the route follows a road to leave by a farm lane which is followed to fields and eventually open moorland and the slopes of Moel Dod and Yr Allt before following a green lane to Tynypant. From here a road is followed for a short distance before joining a farm track onto the ridge walk to the trig point on Ysgwd-ffordd. From here the route drops steeply down about 200m in 0.5km (¼ mile) to Bachell Brook. A minor road is followed to Dyfaenor, which is an old manor house built with stones taken from the buildings of Abbey-cwm-hir.

The route now enters beech woods and eventually a conifer plantation track into Abbey-cwm-hir. Abbey-cwm-hir has a church and village pub and there is also a campsite among the ruins of the abbey.

To begin this section from the crossroads in Felindre turn left and right into a farmyard. Go straight through the farmyard and turn right at the far end of the farmhouse.

Climb uphill, following a track, go straight across at a crossroads and through a gate, which is not waymarked. Continue along the track, through a gate and across a field, staying on the track. Go through the next gate and continue uphill along a newly laid farm track, following the line of trees, to the corner of a field, go through a gate and then follow the track to Rhuvid. Go through a farmyard and climb diagonally uphill.

Map continues p.38

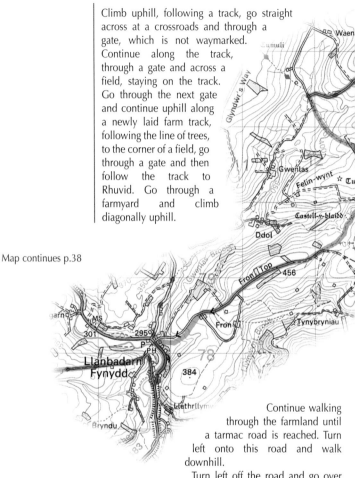

Continue walking through the farmland until a tarmac road is reached. Turn left onto this road and walk downhill.

Turn left off the road and go over the cattle grid, follow the track straight ahead following the waymarks over Gwenlas Brook. The normal red dotted line on the OS map has changed to a line of crosses; this signifies that the track is a BOAT (byway open to all traffic).

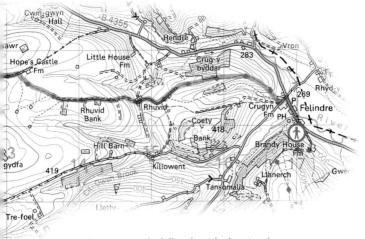

Contour around a hill to the right, keeping a pond on your right, and go uphill to a gate. Go through, continue uphill along a track, which leads into a small wood. Follow the track along the edge of the

Castell-y-blaidd, a medieval Norman defensive enclosure

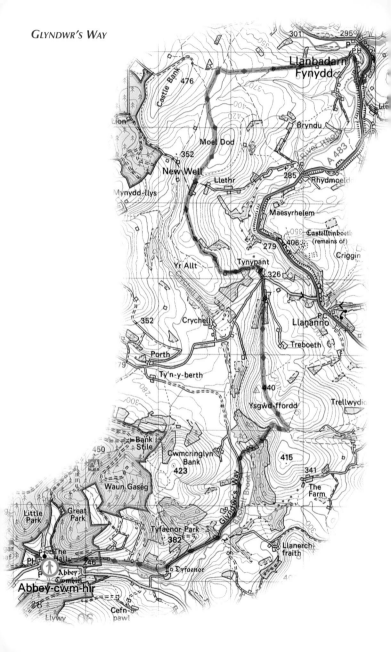

CASTELL-Y-BLAIDD

Castell-y-blaidd translates as 'wolf's castle' and has commanding views to the south and west. This hill fort is thought to have been constructed by the Normans as part of their defences in Wales as several tracks meet in the vicinity. Many place names in Wales refer to wolves, the last known wild wolves in the British Isles roamed the remote hillsides of Powys as late as the 17th century.

wood. The trees are mainly larch and Scots pine, the fallen trees are testament to the ferocious winds on this lonely hillside. Head through a gate at the top of the wood and continue uphill, over the brow of the hill to a waymark post, and from here go downhill to a gate. Go through and bear slightly right, contouring a small hill to a track. Walk across the track and, between the low hill on the left and **Castell-y-blaidd** on the right, follow the indistinct path to a group of trees. Move through a gate and straight uphill, on the brow of the hill bear right to a stile in the fence ahead. Go over and turn right onto a road. After passing a farm on the left, climb a stile in the hedge on the left and turn right and follow the hedge downhill to a gate. Go through this and follow the edge of the field to a gate, go through this, keeping the cattle grid on the right, go down a short lane to a stile, climb over onto the road and turn left to walk down to the A483 and **Llanbadarn Fynydd**.

LLANBADARN FYNYDD

Llanbadarn Fynydd is a small village on the busy A483 trunk road. There are a few houses, a church, a hotel offering guest accommodation and meals, a village store with a post office and a garage. It is thought the area around Llanbadarn Fynydd has connections with the Arthurian Mabinogion tale *The Dream of Rhonabwy,* and that as *badarn* or *badon* means 'mount' in Welsh, this is the Badon Mount in the tale. The area is surrounded by between 20 and 30 earthworks and the village is situated on a Roman road. There is an interesting monument beside the main road erected to William Pugh and his weighing machine!

Ford at Llanbadarn Fynydd

At one time Glyndwr's Way crossed the road here and went through the ford, but today's walkers are spared wet feet and the Way now turns left to follow the A483 through the village, turning right just after the church. Go over the River Ithon, continue up past some houses, around a sharp left-hand bend to a waymarked turning off to the right. Follow the track to a gate and enter a field. Follow the fence on the left through two fields. Careful navigation is needed between here and the slopes of Yr Allt, especially if visibility is poor. Go over a stile and turn left to follow a fence to a stile. Go over this stile and onto common land. Keep to the path through the bracken. The path drops down onto marshy ground, bear off to the right to a wooden footbridge, and then head uphill along a path through the bracken on the slopes of Moel Dod. Continue on the well-waymarked path to a derelict cottage on the left. Cross the stile by the cottage and go down the green lane to a farmyard, go through and continue along the track to a lane. Turn left and take the next turn right. Continue along this road until some woodland is reached. Here there is a waymark on the right. Follow this waymarked path across the top of Ysgwd-ffordd, passing a trig point on the right. The views are wonderful in all directions. Continue down to a waymark and a path to some woods on the right. Take this path through the woods and across a field. Turn left at the bottom, and right onto a lane, over a bridge and up to a road.

At the road, turn left and follow it for 2km (1¼ miles), going past farm buildings on the left. Shortly after this there is a waymark on the right. Take this path through a field into beech woods. Follow the path down over the bridge and bear immediately to the left of a house and go over a stile. Follow a fence on the right and then across a field to the next waymark. Before the house, go through a gate and across a field to the corner of the garden. Bear left, going through a gate in the corner of the field. Follow a forest track to a tarmac road. Bear left and then right at the junction. The road passes in front of a building called The Hall; there is a benchmark in the wall of the grounds to The Hall.

ABBEY-CWM-HIR

Abbey-cwm-hir is a sombre place on a dull day due to the large amounts of forestry plantations on both sides of the valley. The Cistercian monks believed in austerity and hard work and so chose lonely valleys for their abbeys, making them into successful places of industry. They built corn mills, roads, houses, fish ponds and farm buildings. The monks started to build the abbey in the middle of the 12th century. The nave of the abbey was 242 feet long and would have been the fourth biggest nave in Britain – only Winchester, Durham and York being larger – if it had been completed, which it never was.

The Cistercian monks of Abbey-cwm-hir sided with Llywelyn ap Gruffudd in his stand against Edward I. Llywelyn was killed by the English and his head was taken to the King, but his body was buried here. Because the abbey is the last resting place of Llywelyn the Last, it was a shrine for all Welsh people, yet Owain Glyndwr sacked it in 1401, believing the monks to be in league with the English. Henry VIII demolished what was left during the Dissolution of the Monasteries. Five complete arches were taken to Llanidloes to enlarge the church there. Other remains can be found in

Abbey-cwm-hir trout pond

surrounding houses. Little remains of the intended impressive building or of the other monastic buildings. This is a remote part of Wales and the monastery would have needed to be self-sufficient and had its own farm, mills and bakehouse. Walkers can camp among the ruins beside the Clywedog Brook from which the Cistercian monks caught fish.

The village has an inn boasting the uncommon name of Happy Union Inn with a very unusual inn sign. The church here was built in 1866 when the original church, built in 1680, became derelict and had to be demolished. The church was funded by the sister of the local squire. The lych-gate was erected in her memory in 1900. There are some unusual head stones in the churchyard including two War Graves Commission memorials and painted cast iron head crosses.

Benchmarks were cut into rock or stone, usually on churches or other buildings that would not be pulled down and indicated a known height or level on a line of levels. Mapmakers used them by fitting an angle-iron into the horizontal notch as a 'bench' or support for their levelling-staff. The broad arrow was the sign of the War Department (forerunner of the Ministry of Defence) that originally controlled the Ordnance Survey. The standard of Owain Glyndwr is normally hoisted on the flagpole in the grounds of The Hall.

On the left is a metal fence with a gate. Go through the gate and down to the abbey ruins at **Abbey-cwm-hir**.

SECTION 3

Abbey-cwm-hir to Llanidloes

24.5km (15¼ miles)

Map required:	OS Landranger 136
Height gain:	400m

The start of this section is strenuous, climbing from Abbey-cwm-hir at 200m to Upper Esgair Hill (400m), over exposed upland pastures. The route leaves Abbey-cwm-hir by climbing steeply up through a conifer plantation before descending to Clywedog Brook and contouring the hillside before ascending to high pastures on Upper Esgair Hill. A rough moorland track is followed to Bwlch-y-sarnau.

After Bwlch-y-sarnau the route becomes more gentle and drops down to skirt Bailey Bog, though this is along a difficult path. The route now enters and exits conifer plantations several times before reaching sheep farming and pasture land to Berth-lwyd Coppice. After this a country lane is followed for about 2.5km (1½ miles) to Llanidloes.

There are no facilities along the route but Llanidloes has all the facilities walkers need, a post office, banks, bakers and grocery stores and a chemist. There is also a museum and a tourist information centre.

Leave Abbey-cwm-hir by turning right opposite the Happy Union Inn. Follow the green lane beside a fence; do not follow the farm track. Keeping the fence on the right, walk towards a gate and go through it to enter a wood. Follow the track to a crossroads, go straight across and downhill through the woods. Turn right at the bottom and head towards a footbridge. Cross the footbridge over the Clywedog Brook and follow the line of a hedge and a fence to a gate onto a road.

Turn left onto the road and almost immediately right off the road over a stile. Cross a footbridge on the right

and walk to a spur of a hill straight ahead. Map continues p.47
Then bear diagonally left towards a farm, cross a stream below the farm buildings, keeping the buildings on the left, and go across a small paddock to a stile. Climb over the stile and keep a house on the left to go over a cattle grid and follow the track to a stile on the right. Go over the

stile, head diagonally left down the field towards a row of trees, pick up a track which leads down to Clywedog Brook, which is crossed. Go over a stile onto a track, follow this track a short way to a road, turn left onto the road, and go through a gate and up a farm drive. At the farm go through a gate and around to the right onto a track. Continue on the track uphill through two fields, go through a gate

45

and then through a gate diagonally across on the right, leaving the track behind.

Keeping a hedge on the left cross two fields and go through a gate on the left onto a farm track, turn right uphill along the track. Go through a gate into a field and go diagonally right to a gate in a fence, go through, turn left and follow a fence to a gate

Stained-glass window in Abbey-cwm-hir church

46

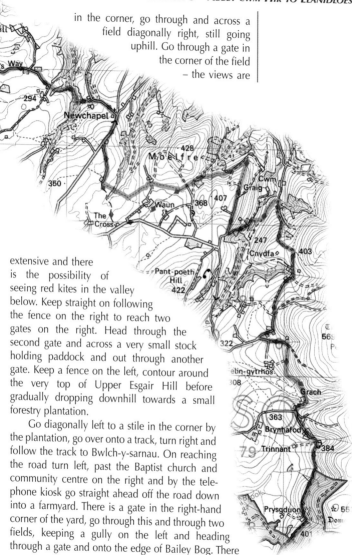

in the corner, go through and across a field diagonally right, still going uphill. Go through a gate in the corner of the field – the views are

extensive and there is the possibility of seeing red kites in the valley below. Keep straight on following the fence on the right to reach two gates on the right. Head through the second gate and across a very small stock holding paddock and out through another gate. Keep a fence on the left, contour around the very top of Upper Esgair Hill before gradually dropping downhill towards a small forestry plantation.

Go diagonally left to a stile in the corner by the plantation, go over onto a track, turn right and follow the track to Bwlch-y-sarnau. On reaching the road turn left, past the Baptist church and community centre on the right and by the telephone kiosk go straight ahead off the road down into a farmyard. There is a gate in the right-hand corner of the yard, go through this and through two fields, keeping a gully on the left and heading through a gate and onto the edge of Bailey Bog. There are a great number of deep drainage ditches here so care must be taken. Aim to the right of the nearest conifer plantation and then straight ahead to a plantation in the distance. There is no well-defined path but there are two waymark posts. The path eventually comes to a forest track; turn right onto this and into the forest. Turn left onto a road and right at the T-junction. ◄

Bwlch-y-sarnau is a high, windswept hamlet, which has a telephone kiosk and a postbox. There are no other facilities, but the views are magnificent. The fortunate walker may see red kite in the vicinity.

Go past Waun Farm. Keep to the road through the forest until two forest tracks come in on the right. Take the track heading north to Prysgduon. Continue on this track to Brynhafod and then follow a road, contouring around the hill, heading towards Grach Farm. Follow the direction of the waymark past the farm buildings, downhill and over a stream. Bear right behind a farmhouse and follow the waymarked route. Keeping a fence on the left, follow the path, left, downhill and turn left onto a road.

At the T-junction turn right, follow the road past a

The windmills of Rhydd Hywel

farm, bearing left. Continue uphill and follow the waymarks, which then point left, downhill. Turn left at the bottom of the hill. Follow the path along the valley bottom and then cross a stream, turn left, follow the hedge on the right to a gate, go through and uphill to a stile. Climb over and turn left onto a track, follow to a minor road and turn right and uphill. The tarmac deteriorates into a track, go over the cattle grid. Go straight on at the Y-junction, following a hedge on the left. Over to the right is Rhydd Hywel Wind Farm. ▶ Keep straight on with a fence on the left.

Walk through the first gate, follow the fence to the right, go downhill to a waymark, turn left along a track, past a cottage, cross a stream and continue contouring on the track. At the junction in the tracks turn left, heading uphill, noting the strata in the exposed rocks on the left. Just before the track goes through a gate turn right, off the track, and go through a gate. Turn immediately left to a stile, go over and bear slightly right to a waymark field post. Go straight ahead to a stile, go over, turn right to a gate in the corner of the field, go through and cross a narrow field to a gate, go through this and turn left. Follow the fence to a stile, go over and turn diagonally right over the brow of a small hill. Walk slightly left to the trees and head through a gate entrance (no gate) to turn right then immediately left onto a farm track.

Turn right before a cattle grid, go through a gate and follow the fence and trees on the left through two fields. Go through the break in a hedge in the corner of the second field, turn right and follow an ancient hedge line, gradually dropping downhill into a sunken path, which goes into a wood. Turn left downhill through the wood, over a bridge (note the old bridge beside the new one). Turn right uphill to come into a field, follow a fence and hedge on the right through a break in the corner of the hedge and straight through the next field, keeping the hedge on the right, to a gate. Go through, turn right onto a road, and follow this to a Y-junction. Turn right downhill and take the next junction left past the chapel at **Newchapel**.

Rhydd Hywel wind farm has 103 turbines and when it was built it was the largest in Europe. The wind farm produces 350 kilowatts of power; enough to supply 25,000 homes – more homes than exist in the whole of Montgomeryshire!

NEWCHAPEL

Newchapel belies its name, not being new at all! It is first and foremost a farming community and is not a village. The scattered houses and farms suggest an older way of life in Wales, when such communities were common. The chapel itself is the focal point where a scattered community can meet on a weekly basis on Sundays.

The first chapel, built in 1740, had a chequered history. It was rebuilt in 1815 and restored in 1905. In 1954 it burnt down, leaving nothing but the walls. It took three years to complete the rebuilding of the present chapel. The graveyard has been used since the founding of the chapel.

Follow the road downhill to a farm. Turn left and go through the farmyard and then turn right immediately through a gate and follow a lane, downhill and across a stream. Then head up through an oak and beech wood, following the signposts. At the top of the woods follow a hedge on the left and a stream on the right. Gradually descend a slope to the stream, which is crossed and head up to a gate. Go through the gate and bear diagonally left across a field to a stile. Go over the stile and onto a road.

Newchapel

Follow the direction of the waymark to **Llanidloes**. On the outskirts of Llanidloes, follow the waymark to the left and take the first turning right through some houses and over a footbridge. Keeping the houses on the left, follow the pavement to a T-junction. Turn right and arrive in the town centre.

LLANIDLOES

Llanidloes is the first large town on the Way after leaving Knighton. The town boasts all the facilities a walker requires: hotels, guest houses, post office, banks, a launderette and a multitude of shops and cafés. It is the first settlement down the River Severn from its source, at a point where it meets the River Clywedog. The town owes its existence to the woollen and weaving industries that abounded in this part of Wales during the 18th and 19th centuries. The town also supplied men to work the Dylife, Bryntail and Van lead mines.

Most of the architecture is Georgian and Victorian but the Market Hall, in the middle of the town, was built in the early part of the 15th century and is open to the public. It is the only building of its kind in Wales to have survived. The lower, open part of the building was used for market stalls, whilst the first floor was used for a variety of purposes. The nave of the church of St Idloes was built with stone removed from Abbey-cwm-hir at the time of the Dissolution of the Monasteries.

The Welsh had been stifled by the Anglican Church so when nonconformists started to travel into Wales, people flocked to listen to them. This resulted in the establishment of a number of different religions in the towns, villages and hamlets, and a variety of different chapels were built: Methodist, Quaker, Baptist and Zionist. John Wesley is said to have visited Wales over 40 times during his lifetime and came here to Llanidloes at least four times.

The local museum off Great Oak Street is worth a visit for its unusual display of a black lamb. The museum also describes the history of the town with many worthwhile exhibits. It is not easy to find, from the Market Hall go up Great Oak Street, past the Town Hall and immediately turn left down a narrow street: the museum is about halfway along the street.

SECTION 4

Llanidloes to Glaslyn

24km (15 miles)

Map required:	OS Landranger 136
Height gain:	740m

This section's route is very varied, passing through deciduous wood, farmland, old mine workings and rough pastureland on the banks of the reservoir as well as small sections of Hafren Forest and open and exposed moorland with many old, unnamed mine workings. The climax is the gorge and waterfall of Afon Clywedog and the flat plateau of the wildlife nature reserve at Glaslyn.

The area is sparsely populated and very exposed with winds sweeping in over the Plynlimon range of hills. Total height gained is 740m approximately, the highest point being about 450m at Glaslyn.

The route follows a road out of Llanidloes and joins the Severn Way Walk through Allt Goch Wood onto a golf course before joining a lane and then crossing a series of fields with views over to Van and its two chimneys. Eventually you join the B4518 which is followed for about 0.5km (¼ mile). A farm track is followed down to the Clywedog Dam and Bryntail Mine, before ascending to the view point of the dam. Another short stretch of road walking brings you to the start of the nature trail, which is followed to the water's edge before you leave it to follow the edge of the reservoir to the sailing club. After skirting the shores of the reservoir, the Way continues through farm fields, conifer plantations and rough farmland to the high ground above Dylife.

You can drop down to Dylife for an overnight stay or to visit the Star Inn. This is the last opportunity for refreshments on this and the next section before Machynlleth. Otherwise, the track above Dylife follows an old Roman road and passes a Roman fortlet at Penycrocbren. Continuing across moorland, the route contours above the Clywedog Gorge passing old mine workings. The area is full of old mine shafts and workings with mine adits visible in the side of the hill. At the head of the Clywedog Gorge the Afon Clywedog tumbles down in a waterfall, which is impressive after heavy rain. The route now climbs up onto the flat plateau of Glaslyn with Foel Fadian in the distance.

From the Market Hall in Llanidloes walk down the main street to Long Bridge. Cross the bridge and almost immediately turn left uphill. After the cul-de-sac on the right called Tan-yr-Allt turn right onto a path, keep on this path into Allt Goch woodlands (the route is also part of the Severn Way). The path joins a track running through the woods, join the track and continue uphill into a clearing, bear right and contour around the hill through the wood. After 100m take the second path on the left, diagonally up through the woods, crossing another path to a fence, go through and continue in the same direction. Eventually the wood thins out and the path follows the edge of a golf course on the left, passing a farm and reaching the Golf Club House. Go through the fence, turn right, walk over a cattle grid and onto a road. Go left off the road at the Y-junction, passing a house on the right and between outbuildings, continue straight ahead on the track and take the right-hand gate of two gates. Follow the track and turn left through a gate into a field. **Van** is spread out on the far hill in front; many of the mine workings can be spotted including the chimneys. Follow a hedge on the left through two fields, go over a stile, bear right and cross a field, go through a gate and turn

Llyn y Fan from the B4518

53

right onto a tarmac road. At the junction turn left and immediately right over a stile, keeping the hedge on the left go through four fields, to a gate onto a road.

Cross the road and up the farm drive of Garth Farm. Before the farm is reached there is a belt of trees on the right, go up the clearing on the edge of the trees onto a farm track. Turn right and follow the farm track through three fields, bearing off to the right before the summit of the hill

Map continues p.57

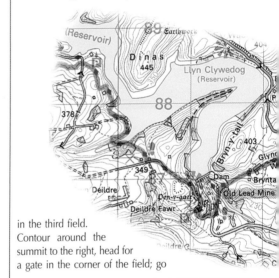

in the third field. Contour around the summit to the right, head for a gate in the corner of the field; go

VAN

Van was at the centre of an extensive area of open cast lead mining. The mines were first worked about 1850 and were the most valuable lead mines in the county with the ore (galena) containing 11oz of silver per ton. At the height of production 450 tons of lead were produced a month yielding a profit of £36,000 per year, with approximately 500 people being employed. A private railway line was built to take the lead and silver from Van to Caersws, a considerable improvement on the farm wagons used by other mines in mid-Wales.

through and into a green lane. Go through the gate at the end of the lane and diagonally left across a field to cross a footbridge and climb a stile in the corner. Keeping the hedge on the left and just before the corner climb over a stile on the left, turn right up the edge of this field, keeping the fence on the right. Go over a stile in the corner of the field and turn right onto the B4518. Follow this road for 1km (½ mile). After admiring the view down the valley towards Llyn y Fan and Van, turn left onto a farm track.

Follow the track down through a farm and out into a field. Keep to the top of the field to the next signpost. At this signpost, either go down through the woods, or turn right and down a track to the bottom of

Bryntail Mine
Originally the area was mined for lead ore, producing 384 tons per month at the height of production, but from 1869 to 1884, when the lead ore mine closed, the emphasis was placed on mining and processing barytes which was used in the manufacture of paint.

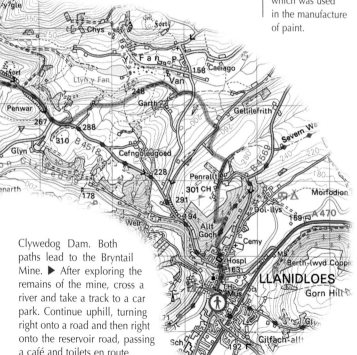

Clywedog Dam. Both paths lead to the Bryntail Mine. ▶ After exploring the remains of the mine, cross a river and take a track to a car park. Continue uphill, turning right onto a road and then right onto the reservoir road, passing a café and toilets en route.

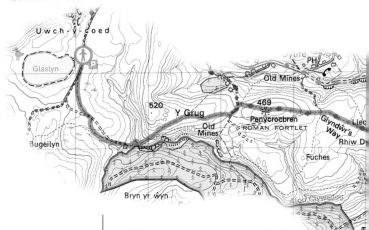

Llyn Clywedog was created in the 1960s, mainly to control the waters of the River Severn in order to prevent flooding further down river. However, the dam also supplies water to local communities and industry in the south and west midlands. Many people fish and sail on the reservoir; nature trails have been developed and there is an archaeological trail around the Bryntail Mine. Above the dam are toilets and a café.

Follow the road and then turn left. ◄

At the hairpin bend turn right over a stile. Climb uphill following an old wall to the road. Turn right onto the road and follow the road to the start of the Scenic Trail. Follow this trail to the reservoir, turning left away from the trail on reaching a small inlet. Follow the inlet around and through the Clywedog Sailing Club, turning right off the track after the cattle grid. Follow the path through the wood and across a field to join a track which is followed to a road. Go straight across the road and through a gate, follow a field track through three fields until it peters out, continue contouring around the hill to a belt of trees. Go through the trees, through a gate and across a field; pass through an old hedge line and continue straight ahead before bearing right, downhill towards a stream. Cross the stream in the corner of the field and head left through a gate into a forest plantation. This is the first of two occasions on which the route enters **Hafren Forest**. Follow the forest track uphill to a stile, go over and turn

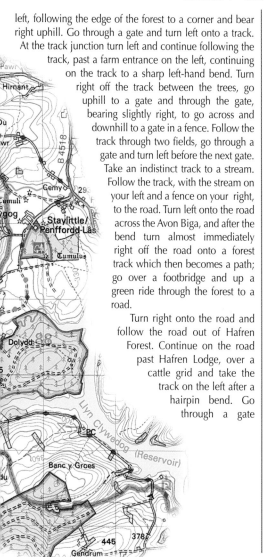

left, following the edge of the forest to a corner and bear right uphill. Go through a gate and turn left onto a track. At the track junction turn left and continue following the track, past a farm entrance on the left, continuing on the track to a sharp left-hand bend. Turn right off the track between the trees, go uphill to a gate and through the gate, bearing slightly right, to go across and downhill to a gate in a fence. Follow the track through two fields, go through a gate and turn left before the next gate. Take an indistinct track to a stream. Follow the track, with the stream on your left and a fence on your right, to the road. Turn left onto the road across the Avon Biga, and after the bend turn almost immediately right off the road onto a forest track which then becomes a path; go over a footbridge and up a green ride through the forest to a road.

Turn right onto the road and follow the road out of Hafren Forest. Continue on the road past Hafren Lodge, over a cattle grid and take the track on the left after a hairpin bend. Go through a gate

HAFREN FOREST

The River Severn was called Sabrina by the Romans and Hafren by the Welsh. Glyndwr's Way only briefly passes through this enormous forest, which covers approximately 52 sq km (20 square miles) on the hills of the Cambrian Mountains. Away to the west is Plynlimon (Pumulumon in Welsh), the highest point of the Cambrian range. On the slopes of Plynlimon are the sources of the Severn, Wye and Rheidol rivers.

There is a mythical story told about the origin of these rivers: Father Pumulumon had three lovely daughters, Hafren, Wye and Rheidol, from whom he did not wish to be parted. However, when he at last made up his mind that they should leave home, he said he would give to each of them all the land between their home on Pumulumon and the sea that they could cover between dawn and dusk of one day. When the day arrived for the sisters to leave, Hafren awoke early and slipped quietly away taking the longest route to the sea. Wye awoke and, having found that her sister had already left, hurried after her. Rheidol overslept. When she eventually awoke she realised that she would have to hurry to get any land at all, so turning in the opposite direction to her sisters, she went rapidly downhill to Aberystwyth ... which is why the River Severn winds about so much and is the longest river in the British Isles, the Wye River takes the prettiest route to the sea and the Rheidol River goes in the opposite direction covering the least amount of land.

and follow the track, go through a second gate and continue straight ahead. Before reaching the stream bear left, past the small waterfalls to a bridge and cross the stream over the bridge. Go up the bank, over a stile to a farm track, turn left onto the track, go uphill to a junction in the track, and turn right to a gate. Go through the gate and follow the track, when it peters out keep the fence on the right, at the corner of the fence go downhill, diagonally right, to a gate in the hedge, go through and turn left to the corner of the field, go over a stiled footbridge, follow the line of telegraph poles through two fields, go through a gate and pass in front of a farmyard. Go through a gate, keeping the farm on the left and enter an old green lane. At the end of the green lane go through two gates, bear left and follow the fence on the left to a corner of a field, go through the gate, bear right to climb

Clywedog Gorge

a stile, drop down the bank to join a farm track. Turn left onto the track, go through a gate and over a bridge across Afon Clywedog, turn left off the track and diagonally right, uphill, keeping the farm buildings on the right. Go over a stile and across a lane, go over another stile and up a green lane. Just before the top of the green lane turn left and go over a stile, heading diagonally right across the field to a stile. Continue uphill, keeping straight ahead to a stile in a fence; go over this and turn left.

The route now joins an old Roman road, first through fields and then across open moorland to a Roman fortlet, which is quite distinct. ▶ (If you are leaving the trail to

Penycrocbren means Gallows Hill and is so called because the execution of the village blacksmith for the murder of his wife and daughter took place here. There is also a Roman fortlet on the hillside.

59

go to **Dylife** take the track on the right downhill just before the open moorland. There is a waymark sign indicating a bridleway to Dylife.)

DYLIFE

Dylife was once a busy lead-mining village, with a population of over 1200. The lead mines have been worked since Roman times and there was housing for the mine workers and their families, a school and church, a 50 foot water-wheel and four inns. However, almost all that remains now are the spoil heaps, a few very scattered houses and the Star Inn. Glyndwr's Way does not go through Dylife but the Star Inn offers overnight accommodation and refreshments.

Star Inn, Dylife, which offers a warm welcome to walkers

After the fortlet continue straight ahead to a farm track and turn left onto it and at a Y-junction take the right fork. The track dissects an old field boundary at this point. Turn right through the gate. Follow the field boundary uphill, keeping it on the left, until the field boundary goes sharply downhill. Then leave it and contour around the hill to a gate. Go through and

Silhouette of Foel Fadian at sunset

continue contouring along an ill-defined path above a dramatic gorge. Remains of an old adit can be seen behind in the hillside. The path slowly descends, still contouring around the hill, dropping quite sharply down to a stream. Cross over using the footbridge and head through a gate and stop to admire the waterfalls before taking the narrow path uphill. Turn right to a corner in a fence, turn left and follow the fence to a stile, go over and up the track. On the right there is a memorial stone in memory of Maurice Jones Griffiths of Nantyfyda, who 'was happiest spending his time in this place'.

At the Y-junction take the left fork past old mine workings on the left; it is dangerous to explore these workings because of unmarked shafts and unstable spoil heaps. These workings were quite extensive – further up the valley on the left can be seen a large embankment which probably formed a dam to a reservoir which would have supplied large quantities of water to the mine and its workings.

Continue along the track to a T-junction, turn left. Foel Fadian, the highest point in Old Montgomeryshire, is now visible ahead. After approximately 90m turn right onto a faint track, this leads to a waymark post with Foel

Fadian straight ahead. Continue walking in a northerly direction towards Foel Fadian until a track is reached, turn right and follow the track past **Glaslyn** to a waymark on the left.

GLASLYN

Glaslyn, which means 'blue lake', forms part of the Montgomery Wildlife Nature Reserve. Like many lakes in Wales it is said to be bottomless and it contains no fish because of the high content of acid in the soil. Arrowheads have been discovered on the northern shore of the lake and an Irish pot, dating from 1000BC, has been found in the vicinity. The pot is in the National Museum of Wales, Cardiff. The discovery of this pot suggests to historians that the Irish actually had a settlement here and that they were not just passing through.

SECTION 5

Diversion – Glaslyn to Hyddgen

17km (10½ miles)

Map required:	OS Landranger 135
Height gain:	230m

This is a mountain valley walk and is optional but provides the opportunity of visiting the Hyddgen Valley, which is the assumed site of Glyndwr's remarkable fight against the much larger Flemish force sent from south Wales. The Covenant Stones of Glyndwr were placed here some time later as a reminder of the battle.

The total height gained and lost on this section is 230m, with the outward route taking you downhill and the return leg bringing you back uphill to Glaslyn. The route follows the Afon Hengwm so it can be very marshy but there are numerous sheep tracks that can be followed. After Bugeilyn there are several derelict farmsteads but little else and so the area is very isolated, providing opportunities for seeing red kites and birds of prey.

On the track running parallel with Glaslyn turn left and follow this track through the nature reserve to a derelict cottage at Bugeilyn. Pass in front of the cottage and continue on the track over a bridge until the track runs out. Now follow the contours of the hills.

Plynlimon can be seen in the distance. Keep the river (Afon Hengwm) on the left. Be careful not to drop down too close to the river, but at the same time do not go too high up the hillside. Walk down the valley until two derelict buildings are in sight, one on each side of the river. Stay above the first building, bear right and follow the wall to its end. The right of way goes down to the first cottage and crosses the river, but it is easier not to. Again contour around the hills, keeping away from the boggy

Hyddgen Stones mark the site of a famous battle

ground by the river and aim for a rectangular clump of pine trees in the distance.

When parallel with the trees, do not cross the bridge but follow a fence on the left to a track. Turn right onto the track. When reaching a point parallel to GR783897 you will see the two white stones known as Glyndwr's Covenant Stones on the opposite hill.

The stones are so named because Owain Glyndwr raised his standard of a golden dragon on a white field on the summit of Plynlimon, and on the banks of the Afon Hyddgen routed a Flemish army of 1500 men. Beside the Afon

Hyddgen two large boulders of quartz can be found; these are the Covenant Stones of Glyndwr. They were placed there some time after the battle. The stones are 60 feet apart and aligned north to south. Glyndwr is said to have camped on the summit of Mynydd Hyddgen, which is a large circular piece of flat, firm ground.

It is possible, if the river is low, to cross and visit the stones. The landscape will not have changed much over the last 400 years and the battle could not have been fought in this boggy ground but on the slopes of the nearby hills.

From here, simply retrace the route back to Glaslyn to continue on the track past the lake.

SECTION 6

Glaslyn to Machynlleth

20km (12½ miles)

Map required:	OS Landranger 135
Height gain:	450m

This is a roller-coaster route, with many ups and downs before Machynlleth though the total height climbed is only about 450m. After leaving the high plateau of Glaslyn the route goes through a mixture of country lanes, farm tracks, conifer plantations and rough pastureland.

From Glaslyn a track is followed to the base of Foel Fadian, which is the highest point in the old district of Montgomeryshire at 564m. The route does not go to the summit but it can be climbed as a small detour from the Glyndwr's Way route. The route itself contours around the hill and drops steeply down to the valley, losing about 200m of height in approximately 0.5km (¼ mile). The Afon Dulas has its beginnings in the spectacular scree slopes below Foel Fadian.

There is then a short road walk, partly uphill, to join a farm track which is followed downhill, back to the Afon Dulas valley and you eventually climb uphill to the slopes of Cefn Modfedd. Again, the route drops down to Talbontdrain before a long steep climb uphill to a conifer plantation on Rhiw Goch (it is advisable to stop and take in the views behind you before entering the conifer plantation).

The route now generally drops gently down to Machynlleth, first through rough pastureland and then in and out of conifer plantations before dropping down through more rough pastureland to join a track past Bryn Glas. A road takes you to a path in front of cottages and to the Roman Steps, which lead to the outskirts of Machynlleth.

Machynlleth is a busy country town with many shops, hotels and banks. There are also a number of visitor attractions in the town or in the vicinity.

Follow the waymark to skirt the flanks of Foel Fadian, passing a spectacular scree slope. Then drop steeply

Map continues p.69

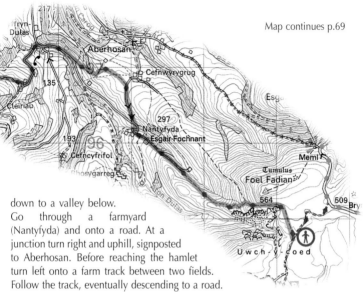

down to a valley below.
Go through a farmyard
(Nantyfyda) and onto a road. At a
junction turn right and uphill, signposted
to Aberhosan. Before reaching the hamlet
turn left onto a farm track between two fields.
Follow the track, eventually descending to a road.

Turn right onto the road and follow it to a telephone
kiosk. Turn left over the Afon Dulas and head uphill to
turn right through the farmyard of Cleiriau-isaf, continue
on the track. At a Y-junction follow the fence uphill; the
track continues through a forest. At a meeting of the forest
tracks go straight across and over a stile, bearing slightly
right to follow a green lane down the side of a field. At a
Y-junction take the right fork, at the farm buildings bear
right and go over a stile. Continue straight ahead on the
green lane, coming out of the woods at the end of the
lane. Keep to the track through the open field, down
through a field, over a stream and up to Talbontdrain. Go
through the yard and turn right onto the road and turn left
onto a track.

Continue on the track, climbing steadily uphill to the
conifer plantation. On reaching the conifer plantation
turn left and follow the edge of the trees to a gate which
you go through. Turn right onto a forest track and descend

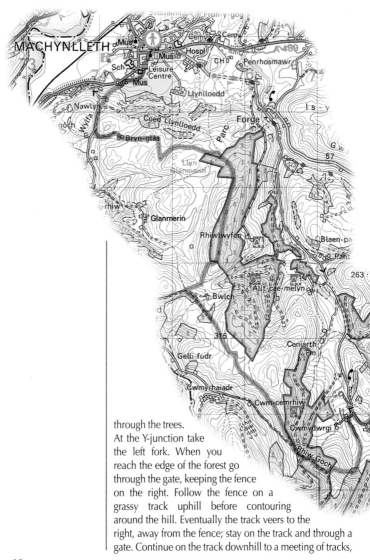

through the trees.
At the Y-junction take
the left fork. When you
reach the edge of the forest go
through the gate, keeping the fence
on the right. Follow the fence on a
grassy track uphill before contouring
around the hill. Eventually the track veers to the
right, away from the fence; stay on the track and through a
gate. Continue on the track downhill to a meeting of tracks,

turn right, head through the first gate, keeping the fence on the right, and follow a rocky outcrop on the left. Go over a stream and shortly after crossing it turn left at the waymark to walk up a steep hill. After a rocky outcrop turn diagonally right and uphill, skirting the summit of the hill, and turn left and enter the forest ahead over a stile.

Follow the forest track and when a track joins from the right keep to the left track. At the crossroads go straight across, still contouring around the hill before gradually going uphill through the forest. At a crossroads go straight across and gradually descend. On a bend a track goes out to the left; turn onto this track and at a stone wall go through the gap and straight ahead to continue along the forest track. Go through the gate at the end of the wood and uphill on a well-defined path; continue on the path contouring around the top of the hill. The path eventually becomes a track and contours around the head of a valley.

At the end of the track go through a gate, keeping a hedge and fence on the right, and head downhill ignoring the track on the left. Follow the track in front of Bryn Glas and at a crossroads go straight across, through a gate and downhill to a road. Turn right onto the road, walking first uphill and then downhill to bear off on a track to the right passing in front of some cottages to a path. Go down an old pathway, descending very old steps that are known as the Roman Steps, and through the kissing gate and turn right, passing The Lodge and walking onto the drive of Plas Machynlleth. ▶ Follow this around the house and into the gardens, bearing right to the leisure centre. Follow the pavement and then gravel path to emerge onto Heol Maengwyn at the Owain Glyndwr Centre in **Machynlleth**.

The Roman Steps probably date from the mid- to late 19th century but the sunken path was originally the main route into Machynlleth. The Romans did, however, have hill top lookouts on the hills of Wylfa and Fron-y-gog between which the town has been built.

69

Looking up the Roman Steps

MACHYNLLETH

Machynlleth, like many Welsh towns and villages, was granted a market charter by Edward I in the 13th century. Machynlleth is laid out on the medieval T-plan, but most of the buildings are Victorian, the blacksmith's forge being given its unusual door prior to a visit by Queen Victoria. Owain Glyndwr held his first parliament in the Parliament House on Heol Maengwyn, not in the present museum, but in an older building probably built on the same site. The clock tower is reminiscent of the one at Knighton, but much grander.

The town, located at a point where the Afon Dyfi could be crossed, has always been a focal point of the area. It developed as a collection point for slate and lead, which was brought down from the quarries and mines in the hills around the town. The Afon Dyfi is tidal just downstream of Machynlleth. A port, Derwenlas, was built to ship the slate and lead ore out.

Later, a railway was built to Shrewsbury, which closed the port because the railway line cut across the entrance to the harbour. This was the beginning of the end of the mining industry. However, the town survived on its woollen industry, producing large quantities of Welsh flannel and tweed. Today its economic activity centres on agriculture and tourism.

Machynlleth, like Llanidloes, has all the facilities a walker requires: hotels, a campsite (at Corris), bed and breakfast houses, cafés, shops, banks and tourist information centre, as well as a post office.

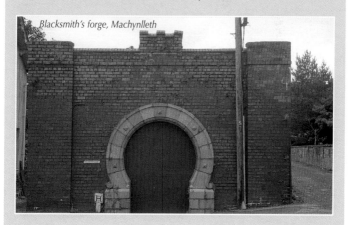
Blacksmith's forge, Machynlleth

SECTION 7

Machynlleth to Llanbrynmair

25km (15½ miles)

Maps required:	OS Landranger 135 and 125
Height gain:	660m

There are approximately 3km (1¾ miles) of road and country lane walking on this section of the route; there are also old green lanes, farm tracks across high ground, rough pastureland and farmland as well as a small section through a conifer plantation. Though the height climbed is around 660m, it is on gentle slopes with the 150m height lost into Abercegir spread over 0.5km (¼ mile).

The A489 is followed out of Machynlleth, through a golf course to Forge and beyond. There is then a very pleasant green track through Pen-rhos-Bach, before joining a country lane into Penegoes. The main A489 is followed for a very short distance to a turn off onto a country road and then farm tracks and fields lead you up to contour the slopes of Bryn Wg into Abercegir. There are no facilities here.

Leaving Abercegir brings an uphill climb out of the village, following farm and field tracks onto Cefn Coch to a green lane. Next is an exhilarating walk through fields, the views are wonderful, dropping 200m down to Cemmaes Road.

A short length of the A470 is followed to a track beside a railway line and the Afon Twymyn. This track and others go up into the hills beyond Commins Gwalia where the Way twists and turns around the hills. Then the route goes through rough pastureland into the Gwern y Bwlch conifer plantation. A forest track is now followed until more rough upland pastures are reached above Llanbrynmair. About 100m of height is now lost in less then 0.5km (¼ mile) as the route goes rapidly downhill to Brynaere and a concrete farm road and a country lane, which crosses the railway into Llanbrynmair.

Llanbrynmair has a hotel, a post office with general store and a campsite about 1.5km (1 mile) outside the village.

Map continues p.74

From the gates of Plas Machynlleth in Heol Maengwyn turn right, turning right again opposite the hospital along the road signposted Llanidloes. Continue through the golf course to Forge. ▶ Turn left over the bridge, go uphill past some houses and take the next turning left. Follow a lane to a Y-junction. Take the right-hand farm track. Go through a gate, across a field and skirt around a derelict farm (Pen-rhos-Bach). Follow a fence to the next gate. Go through this gate and follow the fence to a small wood. Skirt around the wood and go right across a field to a

Forge is a small hamlet beside the Afon Dulas. The postbox, set in the wall of a cottage, is the only reminder of the village store and post office, which closed many years ago.

Mist over Penegoes

Penegoes is a small hamlet on the busy A489. The famous landscape painter Richard Wilson was born here; his father was the vicar of the local church. Felin Crewi, a mill, has been completely restored and produces whole wheat flour. The original mill was built in the 17th century. There are no facilities here other than a post office.

track. Turn left onto the track and through a farmyard. Turn right and, at a lane, turn left. Follow the lane past a restored watermill to the main road at Penegoes. ◀ Turn right onto the pavement.

Take the second turning right off the main road, walk through the village and continue to the end of the lane at Maesperthi. Take the farm lane to the right of Maesperthi and at a junction turn left and go through a gate. Stay on the track through three fields to two adjacent gates. Go through the left gate, turn left and head uphill with the fence on the left. Go over the top of the ridge and drop down to a stile. Go over, keeping the fence on the

right, and contour around Bryn Wg keeping the fence on the right. At the top of a small rise turn diagonally left onto a track, cross the track and go over a stile. Bear left along an indistinct path in the bracken to arrive at a more obvious path; turn right onto this path and continue contouring around the hill before dropping steeply down to Abercegir.

Map continues p.76

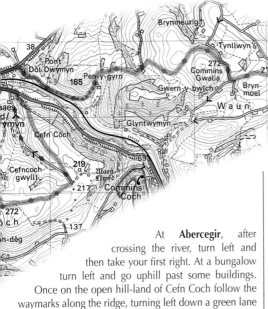

At **Abercegir**, after crossing the river, turn left and then take your first right. At a bungalow turn left and go uphill past some buildings. Once on the open hill-land of Cefn Coch follow the waymarks along the ridge, turning left down a green lane

ABERCEGIR

Abercegir is a charming, peaceful hamlet, which was the site of the last working woollen mill in Montgomery. The Welsh people had always worked the wool of their local flocks of sheep, mainly for their own use. They wove the wool into cloth or knitted it into garments.

This cottage industry produced a surplus, which the farmers' wives sold at local markets in order to supplement the earnings of their men. Gradually this became a major industry in mid-Wales where wool was plentiful, the supply of water was never a problem and labour was cheap.

Newtown was the major centre for the industry, but every town and village had at least one woollen mill, or *pandy* in Welsh. Eventually newer mills were built in the north of England, where the newly discovered coal was used for power, bringing to an end a centuries-old industry.

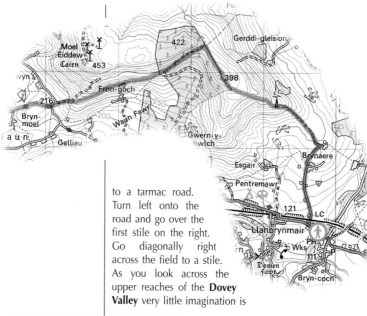

to a tarmac road. Turn left onto the road and go over the first stile on the right. Go diagonally right across the field to a stile. As you look across the upper reaches of the **Dovey Valley** very little imagination is

DOVEY VALLEY

The views from Cefn Coch over the Dovey Valley are spectacular. The original main road along the Dovey Valley can be seen on the opposite side of the valley which passes Mathafran before reaching Cemmaes Roundabout. Glyndwr is said to have visited Mathafran many times in his journeys around Wales. So too did Henry Tudor, the longed-for champion of the Welsh nation, on his way to Bosworth Field. Henry asked Dafydd Llwyd, his host at Mathafran, to predict the outcome of his campaign. Dafydd, not feeling over confident to predict such an important issue, consulted his wife. The sensible woman suggested that her husband should tell Henry that he would win, on the assumption that if he did Dafydd would be well rewarded but if the campaign was lost Henry would not come back to Mathafran. Henry Tudor, by then Henry VII, made Dafydd Llwyd his esquire. The original farmhouse was destroyed by Parliamentary troops during the civil war as the then owner, Rowland Pugh, was a Royalist.

On the opposite hillside is a distinctive depiction of the red dragon of Wales. Mr Hugh Jones laid this out in order to celebrate the second millennium. After two years of planning the project and being thwarted by various planning restrictions, work started on 15 October 1999 and finished on 29 December that year. The Red Dragon of Wales is the oldest national emblem in existence, and was in use before the Romans arrived in the British Isles. The Welsh flag of a red dragon on a white and green background is the only European flag to have a symbol rather than a combination of straight, vertical or horizontal lines.

The Welsh symbol of the red dragon is derived from the legend of Vortigern and Dinas Emrys. Vortigern was an ancient Roman-British king who encouraged the Saxons to come to Britain. However, he fell out with the Saxons and wished to build a fortress to defend himself against them. He chose Dinas Emrys in Snowdonia to build a stronghold but every night the foundation stones laid during the day collapsed. Vortigern's wizards said he must kill a young boy who had a mother but no father and spill the boy's blood on the mortar holding the stones together. Eventually such a boy was found and he was brought to Dinas Emrys. The boy told Vortigern that the stones kept collapsing because Vortigern was trying to build on the site of underground water where two dragons, a red one and a white one, slept. (The Welsh legend of Lludd and Llefelys tells how the dragons came to be under the pool at Dinas Emrys, but that is another story!)

Red dragon across Dyfi Valley from Cefn Coch

Digging proved the boy right but the dragons were none too pleased at being woken and started fighting one another. The red dragon won and the boy predicted this to mean the eventual victory of Wales over England (the white dragon represented the Saxons). The Welsh thus adopted the red dragon as their symbol. The boy, according to Geoffrey of Monmouth, was Merlin, King Arthur's wizard. The red dragon is not so dissimilar to the griffin of the Romans and may have direct links to it; this would make the Welsh flag the oldest national flag on earth.

required to understand why Owain Glyndwr was famed for disappearing and re-appearing when least expected. Across the Dovey Valley is the old coach road, Mathafran and the Red Dragon. Continue downhill through three fields, bearing diagonally right in the next field to a fence and stile; go over the stile, turn left onto a track and walk to a gate. Go through, bear right to a gate and stile, and go over to the A470 which is a very busy main road.

Turn left, follow the pavement to the roundabout at Cemmaes Road, follow the A489 in the direction of Mallwyd, turning off on the right after crossing the Afon Twymyn. Stay on this track following the Twymyn through the valley, gradually climbing uphill and bearing left away from the river and railway. Just before a farm building turn left off the main track onto a grassy path, which goes uphill to the left. When the path peters out bear right, following a fence on the left uphill to a fence and gate in a corner. Go through and bear slightly right to the waymark. Head sharply right uphill to and through a gate and follow a track down to a derelict farm. Keeping the farmhouse on the right go through the yard, and opposite a stone barn turn right through a gate. Follow the track through four fields after which keep the fence on the left to go straight ahead. Pass through a gate and down a grassy track to a road. Turn right onto the road and at a T-junction turn left up an old green lane. It is difficult to know which came first – the green lane or the stream!

At the top of the green lane turn left onto a minor road and on the left-hand bend turn right through a gate. Bear left and right uphill on a track. At the hairpin bend take a look back to retrace the route along the slopes of Commins Gwalia. Continue on the track contouring around Moel Eiddew, entering the Gwern y Bwlch conifer plantation. Continue on the track through the forest to a clearing, take the left-hand track out of the clearing and steadily climb uphill through the forest. Just before a sharp left-hand bend turn right through the trees to a gate out of the forest. Go through. To the left are the wind turbines of Mynydd y Cemmaes. Turn right and follow the edge of the forest to a corner. Bear left across open moorland to a gate in a fence. After pausing to take in the view descend straight down the ridge to the right of the mast. Join the track and descend to a farm, turn right at the farm and continue on the farm access road, crossing the railway line at the level crossing and continuing along the lane to the A470 and the village of **Llanbrynmair**. Turn left to enjoy the amenities of the hotel or local shop.

LLANBRYNMAIR

Llanbrynmair is on the main A470 trunk road. It has a hotel, general store with post office and, about 2km (1¼ miles) from the village, there is a caravan and camping site. Inhabitants of Llanbrynmair used to believe that the man in the moon had been sent there as a punishment for picking up sticks for firewood on a Sunday!

SECTION 8

Llanbrynmair to Llangadfan

17.5km (11 miles)

Maps required:	OS Landranger 125 and 136
Height gain:	400m

This section moves across farmland and lonely bleak moorland, passing through a conifer plantation and along the road of a high valley to moorland, eventually dropping down through farmland to Llangadfan and the A458. A height of approximately 400m is climbed.

The route leaves Llanbrynmair along a country road, turning off onto a track through farmland before climbing uphill through rough pasture and a conifer plantation. The route then follows a road through the lonely Nant-yr-Eira Valley which is about 200m above sea level. On leaving the road at Dolwen there is a steady climb up to the slopes of Pen Coed, an open moorland summit that rises a further 150m, gained over a distance of approximately 1.5km (1 mile). The route then drops gently downhill through farmland to Llangadfan. Llangadfan has a post office, hotel and camping facilities.

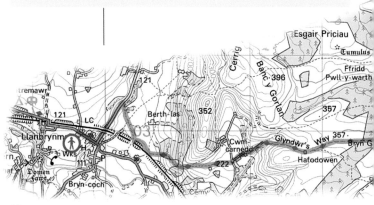

Turn off the A470 beside the Wynnstay Arms, go under Pandy Road Bridge, turning off the road to the right after about 250m. Walk across the field and through a gate, turn left onto the track, just after a gate turn right over a footbridge and stile into a field. Go across two fields, over a stile and footbridge in the field corner, head diagonally left across another field and stile, turn left and go uphill. Turn right at the waymark, heading downhill and over a stile in

Map continues p.82

the wall; the waymarking is poor here and care needs to be taken. Skirt an old barn and cross a marshy field to a gate; go through this and head north-east and uphill to contour around Hafodowen.

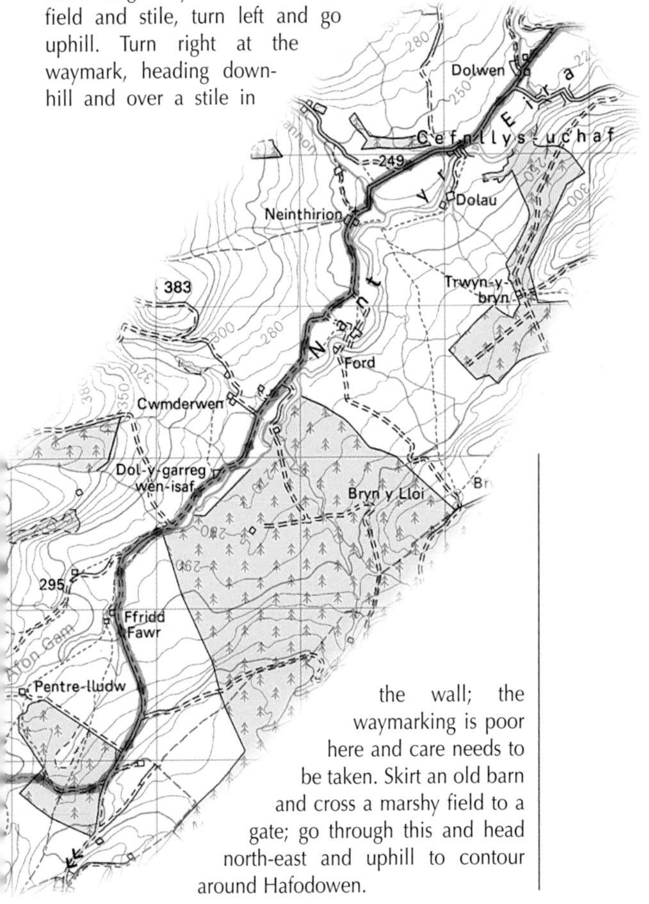

81

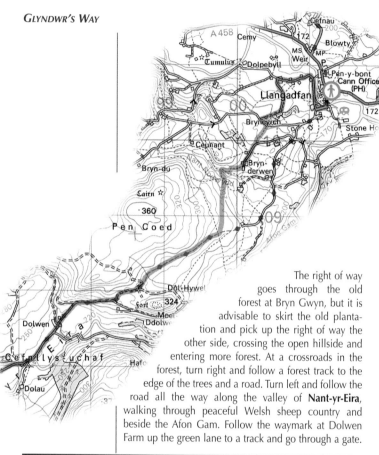

The right of way goes through the old forest at Bryn Gwyn, but it is advisable to skirt the old plantation and pick up the right of way the other side, crossing the open hillside and entering more forest. At a crossroads in the forest, turn right and follow a forest track to the edge of the trees and a road. Turn left and follow the road all the way along the valley of **Nant-yr-Eira**, walking through peaceful Welsh sheep country and beside the Afon Gam. Follow the waymark at Dolwen Farm up the green lane to a track and go through a gate.

NANT-YR-EIRA

Nant-yr-Eira means 'the crooked river through the vale of snow'. The lonely chapel in this valley is a testament to the devotion of this scattered Welsh community. There are mine workings in the valley which were probably worked by the Romans, but could well be older as there have been primitive stone hammers found at the site. The mine, which was mainly open cast, was worked for a considerable time.

Pen Coed above Llangadfan

The green lane turns into a farm track through a field. Turn left through a gate in the hedge and follow the track to the right. At the junction in the track turn left and head uphill. Go through a gate and onto open moorland, keeping straight ahead, and contour around Pen Coed. The hill on the right is Dol-Hywel where the remains of a hill fort ditch can be seen. Ahead in the far distance are Cadair Berwyn and Moel Sych, part of the Berwyn range of mountains.

Gradually descend Pen Coed in a northerly direction to a corner of a fence and, keeping the fence on the left, go downhill to Nant Nodwydd. Cross the stream by the bridge and turn right, bearing left uphill to a gap in a row of trees, go straight across a field and through an ancient hedge line. Follow the path through the rushes parallel with a fence on the right. Go through a gate, cross the track and walk through another gate and bear slightly right across this next field to avoid a pond and then bear left to a gate and stile. Once over the stile, turn left and walk down the road, go over another stile on the left and head straight down the field to another stile. Go over this stile, bear slightly right to a stile in a fence. Go over and bear diagonally right across a field to a further stile to a road. Turn left onto the road and follow this to a farm track on the right, follow the farm track down to a farm and turn left at the end of the farm buildings. Turn left at a road junction and take the turning left off this road to go over a footbridge across the River Banwy in **Llangadfan**. Go past a chapel on the right up to the A458. Turn right for the hotel and village shop.

LLANGADFAN

Llangadfan is a hamlet situated on the A458 with a church, a garage, shop, a hotel and a campsite. The hotel is called Cann Office, which is a corruption of the Welsh name, Cae'n y ffos, which translates to English as 'a fortified field', referring to a hill fort in a field beside the hotel.

SECTION 9

Llangadfan to Llanwddyn

12km (7½ miles)

Map required:	OS Landranger 125
Height gain:	240m

The route leaves Llangadfan along a country road passing through farmland and, after 2km (1½ miles) of road walking, enters Dyfnant Forest along a path and heads onto forest tracks. The route leaves the forest for a little-used road to Ddol Cownwy, which you follow for 1.5km (1 mile). This road is so little used that foxes and badgers use it by day. On reaching Ddol Cownwy the route again enters the conifer plantation although the views above the Vyrnwy Dam are superb. There are many visitor attractions and facilities at the dam.

The route does not cross the dam but takes the road out of Llanwddyn eastwards, before taking a track beside the Afon Efyrnwy, or River Vyrnwy, to the eastern part of Llanwddyn.

Head straight up to the main A458 road, cross the road to go down a minor road past Cross Lane, and at the Y-junction turn left and follow the road to a T-junction. Go straight across and over a stile. Keeping the fence on the left, go across a field, and in the next field keep the fence on the right. At the corner of the fence go straight ahead, following an old hedgerow on the left. Cross a small stream and head up a green lane through two gates and up the side of a field to Penyfford Farm. Pass the farm on the right and onto the B4395. Go across the road and up through the bracken, watching out for the many varieties of trees along this stretch before you enter the conifer plantation. On reaching a main forest track turn left and follow the track contouring around the side of the hill, eventually bearing off right to climb uphill. Llangadfan can be seen behind. Most of the track has forestry plantation on the left and open, rough pastureland on the right. This is the outskirts of the huge **Dyfnant Forest.**

Stay on the track until reaching the point where five tracks meet; bear right and follow a track almost parallel with the main track. Go downhill to another meeting of five tracks, head straight across the main track and bear off to the right, continuing downhill. On the right-hand bend, go straight ahead down an old green track and follow the track and a stream on the right, to another forest track. Go straight across and through a gate. The green lane continues by following the hedge

on the left through two fields. Turn sharp right (the green lane is more like a

DYFNANT FOREST

Dyfnant Forest is an enormous plantation of mixed conifer trees, which include cypress, red cedar, lodgepole pine, Scots pine, Douglas fir, Norway spruce and grands fir. There are also some deciduous trees. The Forestry Commission planted the original forest and it is now managed by Severn Trent Water Company. There are over 64km (40 miles) of forestry tracks throughout the plantation, which covers an area of 2430 hectares (6000 acres). The plantation and surrounding Vyrnwy Estate are havens for a variety of wildlife and part of the estate is a national nature reserve with the local farmers and Severn Trent Water working closely with the Countryside Council for Wales and the Royal Society for the Protection of Birds.

streambed) and keep following the lane downhill. Just before a gate turn left to climb a bank to a bridge, which is crossed.

Follow a forest track a short way through the forest. It leads to a tarmac road. Turn right onto this tarmac road, which follows the edge of the forest to

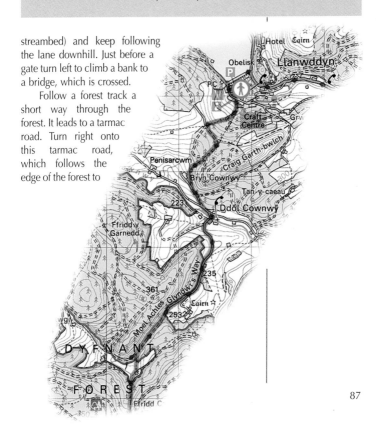

Lake Vyrnwy, which supplies Liverpool with its water

Ddol Cownwy. Turn left immediately after the bridge and left again onto a road at the T-junction at Ddol Cownwy and, shortly after, turn right onto a forest track at a Y-junction. This leads into a different part of the plantation. Follow the track uphill, keeping straight ahead at the first Y-junction but turn right at the next one. At the crossroads in the track go straight across continuing uphill. Keep to the main track round a left-hand bend and at a crossroads cross the track and go over a stile on the right. **Lake Vyrnwy** can be seen from here.

LAKE VYRNWY

Lake Vyrnwy was created in the 19th century to supply water to Liverpool. The dam was the first large masonry dam to be built in Britain and, at the time, it created the largest reservoir in Europe. In order to create the reservoir the old village of Llanwddyn was drowned. When there are droughts, at the far end of the lake part of the lanes and fields around the old village can be seen. Water is sent to Liverpool through massive pipes and is pumped from the Victorian water tower at the side of the lake, using the original pumping equipment. In recent years various visitor attractions have been added around the lake and these include many individual sculptures and a sculpture trail.

Follow the fence on the right downhill, the imposing building on the other side of the lake is the Lake Vyrnwy Hotel. Go to the stile in the corner of the field and climb over, turn right onto a farm track and over a stile in the corner onto a track. Walk straight on downhill on the track which comes into **Llanwddyn** behind the cottages and onto a tarmac road. Turn right, follow the road out of Llanwddyn, and go straight on at the Y-junction. Just before a left-hand bend turn left off the road through a gate onto a farm track. At the end of an old barn bear right, go through a field gate and, keeping a cottage on the right, go through a gate onto a green lane. Stay on this lane to the B4393.

LLAWDDYN

Llanwddyn is a village built in three parts to replace the village drowned by the waters of Lake Vyrnwy. The first part of Llanwddyn you enter caters mostly for the tourist with a café, craft workshops and an RSPB shop. Further on, below the dam, farm and forestry workers' dwellings were built, together with a school and chapel. Further down the river are more modern houses and a new school with a shop and a garage. The church, rebuilt on the hill above the reservoir, is dedicated to Wyddyn, a little known 6th-century hermit who lived in a cave now submerged by the water. There is an interesting obelisk in the churchyard giving the latitude and longitude of the church. The Liverpool Corporation was responsible for the building of the dam and associated works which includes a hotel overlooking the reservoir.

SECTION 10

Llanwddyn to Pontrobert

18km (11¼ miles)

Map required:	OS Landranger 125
Height gain:	300m

This section's walking is easy, following roads and farmland. The route starts on a road but soon joins forest tracks, before following approximately 2km (1¼ miles) of road to Pont Llogel. The banks of the Afon Efyrnwy are followed before the river is left behind as the route crosses farmland to Dolwar Fach. The route moves over open moorland for approximately 1km (½ mile) to skirt the summit of Allt Dolanog before dropping down to the village of Dolanog and following the banks of the Afon Efyrnwy to Pontrobert. There are no facilities at Dolanog but Pontrobert has an inn offering meals and accommodation.

Turn right onto the B4393 uphill to a hairpin bend. Turn right onto a road for Cownwy. Take the first turn left off the road onto a forest track. Follow the track to a junction. Do not turn left at the junction, but continue straight on downhill to a lane. Turn left onto the lane (do not take the forest track that is just before the lane) and follow this lane all the way to **Llwydiarth**.

In Llwydiarth turn right at a T-junction onto a road. Walk along the pavement, past a church and to a bridge, Pont Llogel. Turn left just before the bridge and follow the Ann Griffiths' Walk beside the river, taking the right-hand lower path at the Y-junction. The Ann Griffiths' Walk follows Glyndwr's Way until you reach a stream called Nant Llwydiarth. At the stream cross a bridge and turn left up into a field, following a hedge on the right. At a waymark, go over a bridge and turn left. Continue to the corner of the field, climb a stile and go through this field, keeping a hedge on the left. Go through a gate onto a road. Go straight across the road and follow a farm track, turning left to pass through a farmyard with the farm buildings on the right and the farmhouse on the left. Go through a gate, turn right, and follow a green lane to the next farm. After going through a gate here,

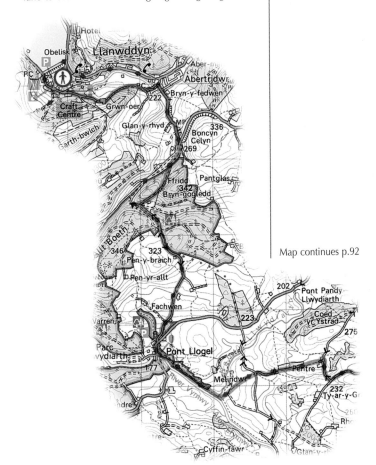

Map continues p.92

turn right, down through the farmyard and then left in front of the farmhouse.

Turn right onto a road and go downhill, over a stream and back uphill again. Take the next turning on the left at the top of the hill. Follow this track through fields for about 1km (½ mile).

Turn right, climb over a stile and go through three fields, over another stile and turn right, following the hedge line down to a stile. Go over, turn left, follow a fence on the left, and in a corner of the field turn right to continue following the fence to a hedge and stile. Climb over the stile and on the minor road turn left. Go uphill, through the gateway of **Dolwar Fach**, the home of Ann Griffiths.

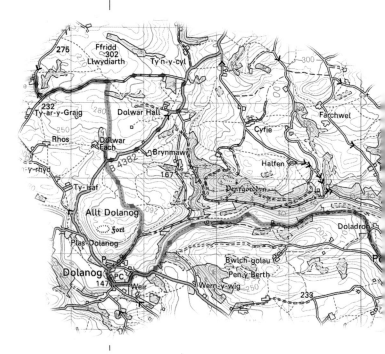

LLWYDIARTH

Llwydiarth has a garage, post office and village shop. The bridge over the River Vyrnwy is called Pont Llogel and the village is often referred to locally as Pont Llogel. In a little park beside a stream there is a carved wooden bench, one of three millennium benches in the community council area of Llanfighangel. The log for each bench came from the same local oak tree which, after felling, was seasoned for about twelve months prior to being cut into three pieces. The local communities of Llwydiarth, Llanfighangel yng Ngwynfa and Dolanog were asked to contribute ideas and designs which would represent local life through local history, local landmarks and nature. Three different local carvers then set about interpreting the various ideas onto the bench seats.

The bench here has many carvings with oak leaves and ivy leaves on the arm rests, sheep on each end and the head of Ann Griffiths, the 18th-century Welsh hymn composer, on the back rest. There is also an upright horseshoe with an anvil in the middle, a small bird and a ram's head. The second bench at Llanfighangel yng Ngwynfa is much simpler with a sheep's head carved into both arm rests and an arched back. Unfortunately Glyndwr's Way does not pass through the hamlet, which is the resting place of Ann Griffiths.

Cross the road and go through a gate. Walk in the direction of two waymark posts. Turn right at the second and cross a stream. Here there are two more waymark posts; one way off to the left on the skyline and one straight in front. Head for the one straight in front and then turn left and head for the second. (If a left turn is taken to go directly to the furthest post, there is a very marshy piece of ground to cross.) On reaching the second waymark, bear right. Do not go straight up the outcrop as the arrow suggests! At the next waymark go steeply downhill, following this path and track to a lane, turn right and then left downhill to reach the village of **Dolanog**.

Looking towards Dolanog

DOLWAR FACH AND ANN GRIFFITHS

Ann Griffiths was born at Dolwar Fach, a small farmstead near Dolanog, in 1776. She was educated at Llanfighangel yng Ngwynfa, a small village school and she was also buried there. Ann lived all her life at Dolwar Fach, never venturing any further than Bala where she went, on foot, to hear Thomas Charles preach his Methodist sermons. Although she had led a very sheltered life, Ann had an extraordinary awareness of human experience and great vision, which inspired her to compose some seventy hymns. Her bible and prayer book were the sole source of her inspiration. The hymns were not written down by Ann but were composed in the tradition of all great Welsh bards. However, the hymns were transcribed after Ann's death by her friend Ruth Hughes of Pontrobert. Unfortunately, it would seem that her hymns do not translate well into English. The Welsh regard her with great affection and many come to visit the area in which she was born and lived. She died giving birth at the age of twenty-nine.

DOLANOG

There is a memorial chapel to Ann Griffiths here. There are also two bridges over the river! There is an Iron Age hill fort on Allt Dolanog above the village, one of many guarding the River Vyrnwy. It is said a giant lived here and controlled the surrounding countryside, but there is also a tale of a dragon who lived on the hill and annoyed the neighbourhood as only dragons can. The villagers were so annoyed with it that they erected a post, which was studded with spikes and wrapped around with red flannel. They then antagonised the dragon and lured it to the post on which it dashed itself in its annoyance and eventually impaled itself and died. This is a familiar tale in this part of Wales and many villages have a standing stone known as Post Coch ('red post').

The third of the millennium benches is passed on the way into the village. One arm rest is carved in the shape of the old bridge with the other arm rest representing the Ann Griffiths Chapel together with a bird of prey. The back rest depicts two salmon, representing the salmon that swim upriver this far to spawn.

Turn left onto a main road out of the village and cross the River Vyrnwy. This road is followed past a water turbine, which produces electricity. At a sharp right-hand bend in the road, there is a stile on the left, which is waymarked. Cross the stile, go diagonally across a field, and take the path that follows the river which goes through a gorge that opens into farmland. Follow the river to Doladron. Having passed Doladron, continue down the track to a road. Bear left onto the road and continue to a T-junction, then turn left into **Pontrobert**.

PONTROBERT

Pontrobert is a small village on the River Vyrnwy. The most noticeable fact about the village is the number of chapels it boasts! One of these, the John Hughes Chapel, was restored in 1995 as a centre for Christian unity, and in memory of John and Ruth Hughes and Ann Griffiths. It is open during the summer months. There is also an inn, a post office and a village store.

SECTION 11

Pontrobert to Welshpool

22.5km (14 miles)

Map required:	OS Landranger 125/126
Height gain:	350m

This section follows farm tracks and paths, with a few short distances on roads. A total height of about 350m is climbed; the high points being Broniarth Hill, with superb views of the Meifod Valley through the trees, and Y Golfa with its 360 degree panorama at about 350m.

Following the road through Pontrobert you join a farm track as you leave the village. The track crosses farmland on paths, tracks and roads on its way to Meifod. A road is followed through the village and over the River Vyrnwy before going uphill through a conifer plantation to the top of Broniarth Hill. After crossing a field you join a road for approximately 1.5km (1 mile) before again crossing farm land to Pant. A road is then followed for about 0.5km (¼ mile) before rejoining farmland and a conifer plantation. There is about 1km (½ mile) of road walking before crossing fields to the golf course at Y Golfa. There are good paths through the golf course before crossing farm land to lanes and roads into Welshpool.

Meifod has two village shops, tea rooms and a hotel, whilst Welshpool is a busy market town with a post office, banks and a large range of shops and accommodation.

From the centre of Pontrobert, head for the bridge. Turn right after the bridge and go past a chapel and an inn. At the inn, take the left road uphill and out of the village. After passing the last chapel on the left, take the next turning right and follow the waymarks along a lane past a cottage on the left. Go through a gate at the end of the lane and turn left onto a field track, go through a gate and turn right, go uphill and at the brow of the hill turn left through a gate. Turn right and follow the hedge to the corner and then turn left to follow a narrow strip of conifers to the next corner. Go over the stile and straight across the field, passing behind a **Quakers' Meeting House**. ◄

Quakers' Meeting House This was originally built in 1700 by the Lloyd family of Dolobran Hall. The meeting house has recently been renovated, unfortunately there is no access from Glyndwr's Way. Charles Lloyd's great-grandson founded Lloyd's Bank.

Turn right and immediately left onto a green lane that goes into another field by way of a very unnecessary stile! Bear right across the field to the opposite corner. Cross a bridge, turn right into a field and follow a hedge uphill to a gate. Go through the gate, turn left and go diagonally across to the next gate. Follow a farm track past a farm, bearing left at the waymark to the next hedge where there is a stile. Go over the stile and turn left onto a lane.

Continue on this lane to a junction. Carry straight on at the junction and head downhill to a farm road on the left, go over a stile in the hedge by the farm road and follow the hedge on the right, heading uphill. Go over a stile in this hedge onto the road, continue uphill, and at the T-junction go straight ahead and downhill to a stile on the left. Go over the stile and, keeping left, follow a fence through a field, contouring around Gallt yr Ancr. At the corner, turn left and continue along the fence to the next corner. Turn right and follow the fence to a track that leads to a gate. Go through the gate and along the track, through a wood and then downhill to a road. At the road turn right and follow it into **Meifod**. At a junction, turn right and head for the centre of the village.

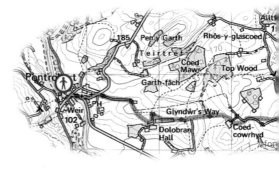

MEIFOD

Meifod has public toilets, a post office, two general stores, a hotel and a garage. It is an important place in Welsh history as it was the centre of both ecclesiastical power and the seat of government for the Princes of Powys. The first church to be built here was in the last half of the 6th century and was the earliest centre for the Christian faith in the area. There have been three churches on the same site. The churchyard is very large for a small village church and the Princes of Powys are reputedly buried here. Mathrafal, the house of the Princes of Powys, is about 2km (1¼ miles) from present day Meifod, on the banks of the River Banwy (just before its confluence with the River Vyrnwy). Little remains of the house except a motte of about 6m (20 feet) in height and 6.5m (22 feet) across, and an enclosure ditch. The Romans may first have settled here and the site may have been occupied throughout the Dark Ages. There are many forts, enclosures and other ancient remains around Meifod, including Gallt yr Ancr, the Anchorite's Hill, which is the probable resting place of Gwyddfarch, who founded the first church at Meifod.

Leave Meifod by turning left along the road between the two chapels, one of which is converted into a dwelling. Cross the bridge over the River Vyrnwy and follow the road to a junction. Take the road on the left that follows the River Vyrnwy and then a path that heads

Map continues p.100

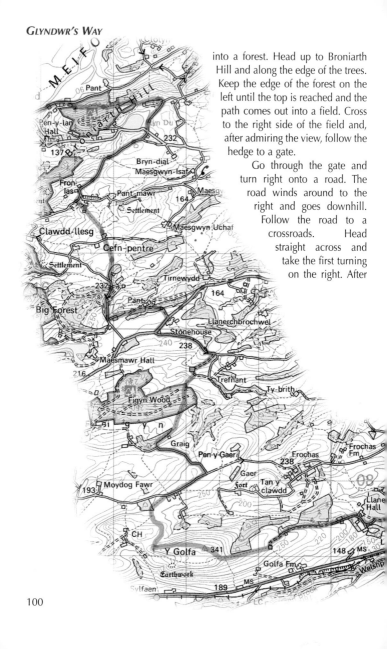

into a forest. Head up to Broniarth Hill and along the edge of the trees. Keep the edge of the forest on the left until the top is reached and the path comes out into a field. Cross to the right side of the field and, after admiring the view, follow the hedge to a gate.

Go through the gate and turn right onto a road. The road winds around to the right and goes downhill. Follow the road to a crossroads. Head straight across and take the first turning on the right. After about 400m, turn left at a waymark and follow the waymarks through fields to Cefn-pentre; the right of way passes to the left of farm buildings. Go through a gate and then alongside the buildings. Turn right in front of the buildings and go out onto a lane.

Cross the lane and climb a stile. Head straight across a field, through some trees and downhill to a gate into the next field. Go straight across this field and over a stile. Head uphill towards a wood and, at the edge of the wood, turn right. Follow the edge of the wood to a stile. Cross the stile, turn left and head uphill.

Follow the road to a wood on the left. Go into the woods and follow a path to a stile. Cross the stile and bear diagonally right up to a fence by a derelict barn. Keep the fence on the right. On reaching a track, follow it downhill to a crossroads. Go straight across and, at a gate, go out onto a road. Turn right and head uphill. At a junction turn right onto the B4392. Take the first turning on the left and keep on this road until just before the farm drive to Trefnant, climb over the stile on the right into a field. Go straight across the field to a fence, follow the fence down to a corner, bear right and follow the line of trees on the right, through an old hedge line and diagonally downhill to the Trefnant farm track. Go

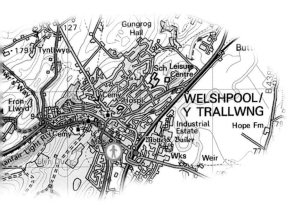

101

Meifod Church

across the track and, keeping the farm buildings on the right, go through a gate and follow a fence down to the corner of the field. Go through the gate and, where the field opens up, turn left going over a brook and climb a stile. Go diagonally right, uphill, to the corner of Figyn Wood. Enter the plantation and follow a stream in a grassy glade between the trees to a junction, orchids grow in abundance in this clearing and deer tracks have been seen in the soft earth by the stream. Turn left and, going uphill, follow the footpath to a forest track – with luck deer may be spotted between the trees. Cross the forest track and continue uphill to the top of the forest. The views on the left are of the Breidden and Moel Y Golfa and behind are the Berwyn Mountains, whilst ahead is Y Golfa.

Go over a stile and straight across two fields to a gate, go through the gate and follow the track downhill to Graig Wood. Turn right off the track to enter the wood, taking care to pick up a fence on the left which is followed to a road. Turn left onto the road and follow it to a T-junction. Turn right and go past a farm and small wood. Turn left off the road at the waymark post and cross a field, keeping to the high ground. Take another left and go through the wood and over a stile onto a golf course. Bear left, follow the fairway to the tee known as The Graveyard. Turn right and head up a steep slope, following a fence up and then downhill to a swampy valley and around to the left and over duckboards. Orchids and bog asphodel grow in this wet hollow. Turn right at the bottom of the bracken-covered slope and follow a path through the bracken, uphill, to turn left and contour around the hill to a junction, turn right and climb up to the trig point on the top of Y Golfa.

There is a 360-degree view from the trig point: in the north are the Berwyn Mountains, the highest of which is Cadair Berwyn; around to the north-east are the quarried cliffs of Llanymynech Hill where there is another golf course. Further round is Gungrog Hill, above Welshpool, and across the Severn Plain, the Breidden and its monument to Admiral Rodney. On a clear day, between

Gungrog Hill and the Breidden, you can just make out the Wrekin on the far side of the Shropshire Plain. Next to the Breidden is Moel Y Golfa and then Long Mountain, which Offa's Dyke climbs up. In the distance you can make out the individual rocky outcrops of the Stipperstones, coming round to the south Corndon can be seen. Just visible in the near distance is the church spire of Castle Caereinion. In the west are the unmistakeable summits of Cader Idris, the Arans and the Arrenigs. You may hear the whistle of a steam train, which is the Welshpool/Llanfair Caereinion narrow-gauge railway below.

WELSHPOOL

Welshpool is the first town of any size since Machynlleth and advantage can be taken of its shops, banks, launderette, swimming pool and other leisure facilities.

At the outset of Glyndwr's rebellion, Welshpool was, in effect, an English stronghold, and the garrison at Powys Castle was able to withstand the attacks made on it by the rebels; only the outskirts of Welshpool suffered any damage. It is apparent, though, that the rebels controlled most of the surrounding area, having won a battle to the north of the town on the banks of the River Vyrnwy, sacked Montgomery and gained successes throughout the area.

The Princes of Powys moved to Welshpool after Mathrafal burnt to the ground in 1212. The building of the present castle started in about 1275. It has many later additions and alterations and is now a National Trust property.

The town is divided by the Montgomery Canal, which brought much wealth to the area before the introduction of the railway and the collapse of the canal trade. Prior to the building of the canal, goods were brought up the River Severn, which is the longest navigable waterway in the west of Britain, to Pool Quay. The Powysland Museum is housed in the Shropshire Union Canal Warehouse and has local history and archaeological displays.

The Welshpool to Llanfair Caereinion Railway was originally opened in 1903 and has been referred to as 'the farmers' line' for the principal freight traffic was farm produce and livestock. Originally the narrow-gauge line joined the standard GWR line at a goods yard, making use of an old tramway through the town streets. The line was closed down in November 1956 but was re-opened in April 1963, by enthusiasts, to passengers.

Howell Park Plinth, Welshpool

From the trig point continue in an easterly direction downhill. At the T-junction turn right and continue following the path downhill. Leave the bracken-covered hillside behind by going through a gate into a field and following the edge of a wood, cross the field to a gate and stile in the corner. Go over the stile and cross a field (note the badgers' holt), in the corner go through a gate into a further field. Cross the field between the hawthorn trees of two old boundary hedges to pick up a track. Follow the track through the field, around an old brick barn on the right and through a gate into a farm lane. Continue along the lane, passing Llanerchydol Hall onto an enclosed track. At a junction continue straight ahead keeping a red brick wall on the right. Go over a cattle grid and stay on the track through parkland, following the tarmac road of the estate down to the roundabout on the A490 at Raven Square, on the outskirts of **Welshpool**.

Take the road to the town centre, walking past some interesting black and white houses, a Victorian wall postbox with a hinged flap, the town hall where another benchmark can be found and a diversion along New Street takes you to the only cockpit in Wales still in its original position. This was built in the 18th century and was last used in 1849 when cock fighting was abolished. Return to Broad Street and go straight across at the crossroads, down Severn Street, over the canal bridge and into a small park (Howell Park) on the left. This is the official end (or beginning!) of Glyndwr's Way.

SECTION 12

Welshpool to Knighton

47km (29¼ miles)

Maps required:	OS Landranger 126 and 137
Height gain:	1100m

Glyndwr's Way ends (or begins) at Welshpool. However, the Offa's Dyke National Trail can be picked up at Welshpool and makes a circular walk back to Knighton. A height of about 1100m is gained and lost, with the highest point being reached on Llanfair Hill (432m). The route uses paths, tracks, farm lanes and roads to reach Knighton. There are many fine views from the high points along the route.

The Montgomeryshire Canal towpath is followed out of Welshpool before joining the A458 for a short distance. The route then crosses farmland up to Beacon Ring (408m) and its magnificent views, before dropping down through more farmland and conifer plantations, where careful navigation is required, to join the course of a Roman road to Forden. There is then about 8km (5 miles) of walking through the flat farmland of the River Severn Plain to Mellington Hall.

After Mellington Hall the route continues south over the east–west grain of the land, first climbing up through farmland to cross the Kerry Ridgeway before dropping down, then up and down to Churchtown. Climbing up from Churchtown the Dyke runs in tandem with the Shropshire Way for about 1km (½ mile), before it heads off to the east. Careful navigation is required just before Middle Knuck Farm where the Dyke appears to be out of alignment. The route follows tracks and paths (with a small amount of road walking) up and down the various hills to reach Panpunton Hill above the Teme Valley and Knighton. Dropping steeply down 120m to the River Teme, you go across and follow the banks of the river, and the Acorn signs, into Knighton.

This is a long and strenuous walk and there are few facilities along the route (just one or two inns at Forden and Brompton). Better facilities are available at Montgomery which is about 1km (½ mile) off the route and at Newcastle about 1km from the route.

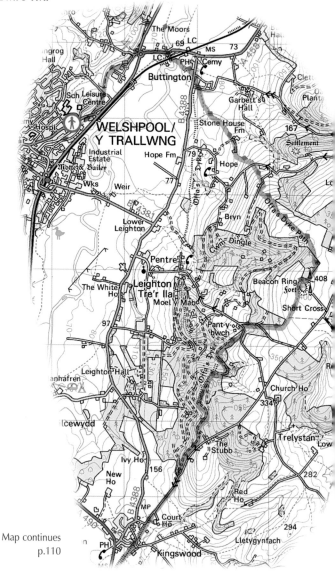

Map continues
p.110

THE MONTGOMERY CANAL

The first stretch of the canal from Lower Frankton to Llanymynech was opened in 1796. It arrived in Welshpool in 1797. The canal was built to transport raw materials into the area, including limestone from Llanymynech, and to export goods out – mainly produce from the woollen mills. In 1936 a breach occurred close to Lower Frankton and it was never repaired, leaving the canal derelict. Parts have now been restored; the stretch through Welshpool was one of the first restoration projects of the Montgomery Canal Society. The wharf between Welshpool and Buttington houses the *Heulwen*, the first barge specially constructed for handicapped people in the country.

Walk across Howell Park to the **Montgomery Canal** and turn right onto the towpath, follow this to Buttington Wharf.

At this point, leave the canal and go up to the road and then turn left and go down to a roundabout. Take the Shrewsbury road off the roundabout and follow it to **Buttington** where there is an Offa's Dyke National Trail waymark on the right. The Offa's Dyke National Trail is joined at this point.

BUTTINGTON

In AD894 a great battle took place here. The banner of the Red Dragon of Cambria was flown at Buttington while the White Dragon banner of the Saxons and the Raven of the Danes could be seen elsewhere on the plain. The Celts and the Saxons came together, forgetting their differences, in an attempt to wipe out the Danish threat in Britain. The battle, when it finally came after months of waiting, was fierce and bloody. Many were killed on both sides but the Danes fled, defeated. When digging foundations for the national school in the north-west corner of the churchyard, many hundreds of human bones were found, a testament to the slaughter that took place.

Take this turn and cross a field and a railway line, taking care. This National Trail can now be followed south to Knighton. The waymarks can all be identified by the National Trail white acorn emblem. Turn right onto a road, and turn off to the left at the waymark.

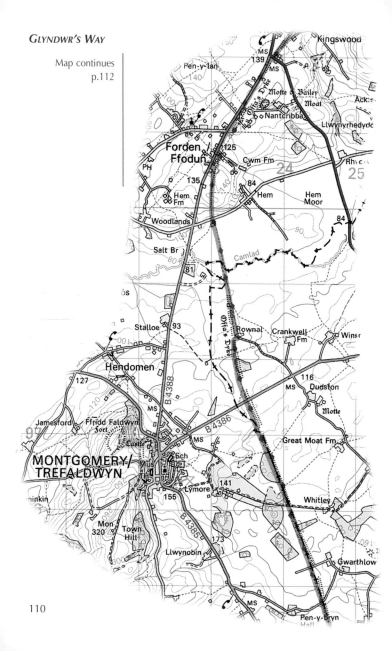

Map continues
p.112

Kingswood

Pen-y-lan

Motte & Bailey
Moat

Nantcribba

Llwynyrhedydc

Forden /
Ffodun

PH

Cwm Fm

Hem
Fm

Hem

Hem
Moor

Woodlands

Salt Br

Camlad

Stalloe

Rownal

Crankwell
Fm

Winsr

Hendomen

Dudston

Jamesford

Ffridd Faldwyn
fort

Castle

Motte

Great Moat Fm

MONTGOMERY/
TREFALDWYN

Sch

Mus

Lymore

minkin

Mon
320

Town
Hill

Whitley

Llwynobin

Gwarthlow

Pen-y-bryn
Hall

There now begins a long, steep climb, mainly through fields, up to Long Mountain, but the views are well worth the effort!

On reaching some masts, follow the edge of the Iron Age hill fort at Beacon Ring round to the left and then right again and continue downhill, following the waymarks.

Offa's Dyke on Llanfair Hill

THE LEIGHTON ESTATE

The Leighton Estate was owned by John Naylor, a great innovator, who developed the estate during the middle part of the 19th century. He built an elaborate system of pools, one of which is Offa's Pool, to provide water to a turbine. The turbine was used to drive mills, chaff-cutting and sheep-shearing equipment and other power-driven farm machinery. He also experimented with bonemeal and guano to provide liquid fertiliser, which was fed to the fields through an irrigation system. He built a model village for the farm workers, a hall with elaborate gardens and a plantation on the estate; the trees include redwoods, wellingtonias and monkey-puzzle. The church and hall were amongst the first in the country to be lit by gas.

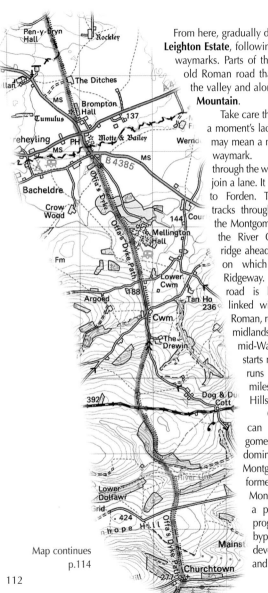

From here, gradually drop down into the **Leighton Estate**, following the white acorn waymarks. Parts of the route follow an old Roman road that comes up from the valley and along the top of **Long Mountain**.

Take care through the forest as a moment's lack of concentration may mean a missed white acorn waymark. Continue down through the wood and eventually join a lane. It is not far from here to Forden. The route follows tracks through farmland across the Montgomery Plain, crossing the River Camlad. The long ridge ahead is the Kerry Hills, on which runs the Kerry Ridgeway. This old drovers' road is believed to have linked with other, possibly Roman, routes from the west midlands to Caersws in mid-Wales. The Ridgeway starts near Newtown and runs for 26km (16 miles) over the Kerry Hills to Bishop's Castle.

Over to the right can be seen Montgomery Castle which dominates the town of Montgomery. This is the former county town of Montgomeryshire. It is a pleasant town that progress seems to have bypassed during the development of canal and rail transport,

Map continues
p.114

THE SHROPSHIRE PLAIN

The Shropshire Plain, through which the River Severn flows, may be one of the richest historical sites in Wales: Iron Age man was present at Caer Digoll or Beacon Ring; the Romans certainly came here (there is a Roman road along the top of Long Mountain); the Breidden is a contender for the site of Caractacus' last battle against the Romans; the site of a ford at Rhydycroes is allegedly where Arthur had his camp in the Arthurian tale *The Dream of Rhonabwy*; Bronze Age Irish pedlars would certainly have used the route through the plain to the rest of Britain; Offa built part of his Dyke here; Cadwallon and Edwin, King of Northumbria, fought here in the 7th century; the Danes were banished from Wales by the joint forces of the Celts and the Saxons in the 10th century; in the 13th century Edward I defeated Madoc here; the Cistercians built Strata Marcella Abbey, which was founded in 1170. The list of events and people that have come this way seems to be endless.

It has also always been a major transport route. Severn trows (local sailing barges) plied up and down the river to Pool Quay until the canal arrived. The A483 is now a very busy road and there is even an airport.

which gave an advantage to the more accessible Welshpool and Newtown. The present castle was begun in 1223, with the medieval town laid out below it. The castle was never captured but chose to surrender to the Parliamentarians during the civil war. The town, however, has been sacked

LONG MOUNTAIN AND CAER DIGOLL (BEACON RING)

Long Mountain is over 300m (1000 feet) above the Shropshire Plain. On the top is the site of an Iron Age hill fort called Caer Digoll, which appears frequently in early Welsh poetry, legends and traditions. For example, it is referred to as the site of the graves of the warriors of the Isle of Britain in *The Dream of Rhonabwy*. It is certainly impressive even with its modern grove of beech trees. The hawthorns encircling the fort may well be descendants of the original hawthorn barrier planted by Iron Age man around the fort, with gorse, to repel wild animals. The views are impressive; Plynlimon, Cader Idris, the Berwyns, the Wrekin and the south Shropshire hills can all be seen plainly on a clear day. Looking down on the Shropshire Plain you begin to understand the importance of this gateway into Wales.

Map continues
p.116

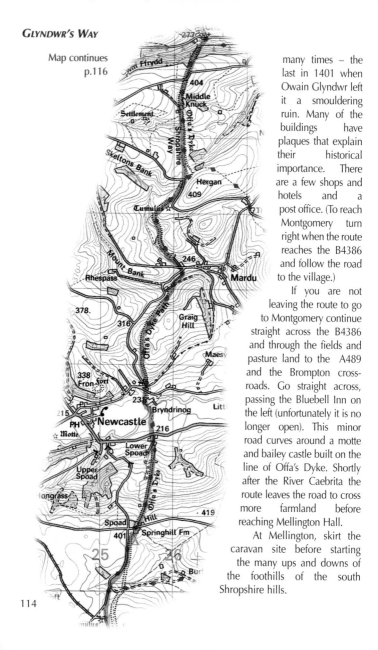

many times – the last in 1401 when Owain Glyndwr left it a smouldering ruin. Many of the buildings have plaques that explain their historical importance. There are a few shops and hotels and a post office. (To reach Montgomery turn right when the route reaches the B4386 and follow the road to the village.)

If you are not leaving the route to go to Montgomery continue straight across the B4386 and through the fields and pasture land to the A489 and the Brompton cross-roads. Go straight across, passing the Bluebell Inn on the left (unfortunately it is no longer open). This minor road curves around a motte and bailey castle built on the line of Offa's Dyke. Shortly after the River Caebrita the route leaves the road to cross more farmland before reaching Mellington Hall.

At Mellington, skirt the caravan site before starting the many ups and downs of the foothills of the south Shropshire hills.

CHURCHTOWN

Churchtown boasts only a church but no town! It is the church of Mainstone some 1.5km (1 mile) to the west. Mainstone was thought to be a border trading post in times gone by and its name was derived from a stone used to weigh the corn both in Welsh (maen) and English (stone). The stone now rests in Churchtown Church and is said to weigh 204.5lbs, the weight of a sack of corn together with the weight of the sack itself.

The first climb up meets the Kerry Ridgeway, which runs west to east and is believed to be the oldest pathway in Wales. Continue south, dropping down to the delightfully named River Unk. A climb up to Edenhope Hill is followed by a descent to **Churchtown**. (Be grateful that the walk is north to south as the descent here is extremely steep!) Between here and Knighton there are many ups and downs. The route climbs Graig Hill and descends into the valley of the River Clun beside the half-timbered building of Bryndrinog. This offers a pause for photographs and reflection on A. E. Houseman's *A Shropshire Lad*, in which he wrote:

> In valleys of springs of rivers,
> By Ony, Teme and Clun,
> The country for easy livers,
> The quietest under the sun.

OFFA'S DYKE

Offa's Dyke was built on the orders of Offa, King of Mercia (an area roughly covering the midlands), in the 8th century. It is thought that the Dyke was principally built to mark the border between the Welsh and English kingdoms. The Dyke runs the entire length of the Welsh Marches, from Chepstow in the south to Prestatyn in the north, although parts have been destroyed. Much of the Dyke corresponds with today's border and crosses into England and back into Wales several times. Some of the most impressive remains of the Dyke can be found along the stretch from Long Mountain to Knighton; note in particular the area about 1km (½ mile) to the north of Middle Knuck Farm, on Springhill and on Llanfair Hill.

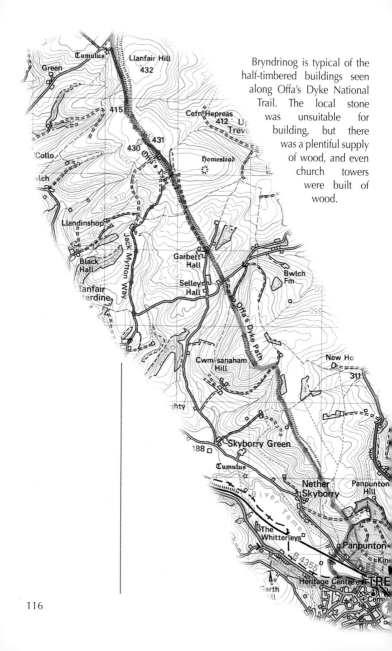

Bryndrinog is typical of the half-timbered buildings seen along Offa's Dyke National Trail. The local stone was unsuitable for building, but there was a plentiful supply of wood, and even church towers were built of wood.

Montgomery Castle to the west of Offa's Dyke

The route continues up Spoad Hill, Llanfair Hill (where **Offa's Dyke** itself is clearly defined), Swm-Sanaham and, finally, Panpunton Hill, from which there is a steep descent to the River Teme.

On reaching Panpunton Farm, go through a field, cross the railway and a footbridge over a river and bear left. Follow the river and the waymarks to the Offa's Dyke Centre. At the centre, turn left down the road to the clock tower in the middle of Knighton, to bring the walk full circle.

117

Knighton Clock Tower

APPENDIX A

Bibliography

Barker, Richard, *Myths and Legends of the British Isles* (The Boydell Press, 1999)

Burnham, Helen, *A Guide to Ancient and Historic Wales (Clwyd and Powys)*, CADW Welsh Historic Monuments (HMSO, 1995)

Gantz, Jeffrey, *Mabinogion Translated* (Penguin Classics, 1976)

Gregory, Donald, *Radnorshire – A Historical Guide* (Gwasg Carreg Gwalch, 1994)

Henken, Elissa R. , *National Redeemer* (University of Wales Press, date unknown)

Lloyd, J. E. , *Owen Glendower* (Oxford Clarendon Press, 1931)

Morris, Jan, *The Matter of Wales* (Penguin, 1984)

Phillips, Pauline, *View of Old Montgomeryshire* (Christopher Davies, Swansea, 1977)

Sale, Richard, *Owain Glyndwr's Way* (Hutchinson, 1985)

Shaw, Joan, *Mostly Montgomeryshire* (K. A. F. Brewin Books, 1992)

Skidmore, Ian, *Owain Glyndwr Prince of Wales* (Christopher Davies, Swansea, 1978)

Stone, Moira K., *Mid-Wales Companion* (Anthony Nelson, 1989)

Housman, A.E., *A Shropshire Lad* (Palmers Press, 1987)

Montgomeryshire Collections (Powysland Club, 1868–1974)

Powys County Handbook (Powys County Council, updated regularly)

Powys Montgomeryshire Village Book, Compiled by Powys Montgomeryshire Federation of Women's Institutes (joint publication between: Countryside Books, Newbury and the Powys Montgomeryshire Federations of Women's Institutes, 1989)

Many local leaflets from churches and local community councils, Powys County Council and the Welsh Tourist Board.

APPENDIX B
Summary of Route

Section	Start/Finish	Approximate Distance	Height Gained	Maps required
1	Knighton to Felindre	25km (15½miles)	600m	OS Landranger 137 and 136
2	Felindre to Abbey-cwm-hir	25km (15½ miles)	520m	OS Landranger 136
3	Abbey-cwm-hir to Llanidloes	24.5km (15¼ miles)	400m	OS Landranger 136
4	Llanidloes to Glaslyn	24km (15 miles)	740m	OS Landranger 136
5	Glaslyn to Hyddgen	17km (10½ miles)	230m	OS Landranger 135
6	Glaslyn to Machynlleth	20km (12½ miles)	450m	OS Landranger 135
7	Machynlleth to Llanbrynmair	25km (15½ miles)	660m	OS Landranger 135 and 125
8	Llanbrynmair to Llangadfan	17.5km (11 miles)	400m	OS Landranger 125 and 136
9	Llangadfan to Llanwddyn	12km (7½ miles)	240m	OS Landranger 125
10	Llanwddyn to Pontrobert	18km (11¼ miles)	300m	OS Landranger 125
11	Pontrobert to Welshpool	22.5km (14 miles)	350m	OS Landranger 125 and 126
12	Welshpool to Knighton	47km (29¼ miles)	1100m	OS Landranger 126 and 137

NOTES

NOTES

NOTES

LISTING OF CICERONE GUIDES

NORTHERN ENGLAND
LONG-DISTANCE TRAILS
The Dales Way
The Reiver's Way
The Alternative Coast to Coast
The Coast to Coast Walk
The Pennine Way
Hadrian's Wall Path
The Teesdale Way

FOR COLLECTORS OF SUMMITS
The Relative Hills of Britain
Mts England & Wales Vol 2 –
England
Mts England & Wales Vol 1 – Wales

BRITISH CYCLE GUIDES
The Cumbria Cycle Way
Lands End to John O'Groats – Cycle
Guide
On the Ruffstuff: 84 Bike Rides in
North England
Rural Rides No.1 – West Surrey
Rural Rides No.2 – East Surrey
South Lakeland Cycle Rides
Border Country Cycle Routes
Lancashire Cycle Way

CANOE GUIDES
Canoeist's Guide to the North-East

LAKE DISTRICT AND
MORECAMBE BAY
Coniston Copper Mines
Scrambles in the Lake District
More Scrambles in the Lake District
Walks in Silverdale and
Arnside AONB
Short Walks in Lakeland 1 – South
Short Walks in Lakeland 2 – North
Short Walks in Lakeland 3 – West
The Tarns of Lakeland Vol 1 – West
The Tarns of Lakeland Vol 2 – East
The Cumbria Way &
Allerdale Ramble
Winter Climbs in the Lake District
Roads and Tracks of the Lake
District
The Lake District Angler's Guide
Rain or Shine – Walking in the
Lake District
Rocky Rambler's Wild Walks
An Atlas of the English Lakes

NORTH-WEST ENGLAND
Walker's Guide to the
Lancaster Canal
Walking in Cheshire
Family Walks in the
Forest Of Bowland
Walks in Ribble Country
Historic Walks in Cheshire
Walking in Lancashire
Walks in Lancashire Witch Country
The Ribble Way

THE ISLE OF MAN
Walking on the Isle of Man
The Isle of Man Coastal Path

PENNINES AND
NORTH-EAST ENGLAND
Walks in the Yorkshire Dales – Vol 1
Walking in the South Pennines
Walking in the North Pennines
The Yorkshire Dales
Walks in the North York Moors –
Vol 1
Walks in the North York Moors –
Vol 2
Walking in the Wolds
Waterfall Walks – Teesdale and
High Pennines
Walking in County Durham
Yorkshire Dales Angler's Guide
Backpacker's Britain – Northern
England
Walks in Dales Country
Historic Walks in North Yorkshire
South Pennine Walks
Walking in Northumberland

DERBYSHIRE, PEAK DISTRICT,
EAST MIDLANDS
High Peak Walks
White Peak Walks Northern Dales
White Peak Walks Southern Dales
White Peak Way
The Viking Way
Star Family Walks Peak District &
South Yorkshire
Walking In Peakland
Historic Walks in Derbyshire

WALES AND WELSH BORDERS
Ascent of Snowdon
Welsh Winter Climbs
Hillwalking in Wales – Vol 1
Hillwalking in Wales – Vol 2
Scrambles in Snowdonia
Hillwalking in Snowdonia
The Ridges of Snowdonia
Hereford & the Wye Valley
Walking Offa's Dyke Path
The Brecon Beacons
Lleyn Peninsula Coastal Path
Anglesey Coast Walks
The Shropshire Way
Spirit Paths of Wales
Glyndwr's Way
The Pembrokeshire Coastal Path
Walking in Pembrokeshire
The Shropshire Hills – A Walker's
Guide
Backpacker's Britain Vol 2 – Wales

MIDLANDS
The Cotswold Way
West Midlands Rock
The Grand Union Canal Walk
Walking in Oxfordshire
Walking in Warwickshire
Walking in Worcestershire
Walking in Staffordshire
Heart of England Walks

SOUTHERN ENGLAND
The Wealdway & the Vanguard Way
Exmoor & the Quantocks
Walking in the Chilterns
Walks in Kent Book 2
Two Moors Way
Walking in Dorset
Walking in Cornwall
A Walker's Guide to the Isle of
Wight
Walking in Devon
Walking in Somerset
The Thames Path
Channel Island Walks
Walking in Buckinghamshire
The Isles of Scilly
Walking in Hampshire
Walking in Bedfordshire
The Lea Valley Walk
Walking in Berkshire
The Definitive Guide to
Walking in London
The Greater Ridgeway
Walking on Dartmoor
The South West Coast Path
Walking in Sussex
The North Downs Way
The South Downs Way

SCOTLAND
Scottish Glens 1 – Cairngorm Glens
Scottish Glens 2 – Atholl Glens
Scottish Glens 3 – Glens of
Rannoch
Scottish Glens 4 – Glens of
Trossach
Scottish Glens 5 – Glens of Argyll
Scottish Glens 6 – The Great Glen
Scottish Glens 7 – The Angus Glens
Scottish Glens 8 – Knoydart
to Morvern
Scottish Glens 9 – The Glens
of Ross-shire
Scrambles in Skye
The Island of Rhum
Torridon – A Walker's Guide
Ski Touring in Scotland
Walking the Galloway Hills
Walks from the West Highland
Railway
Border Pubs & Inns –
A Walkers' Guide
Walks in the Lammermuirs
Scrambles in Lochaber
Walking in the Hebrides
Central Highlands: 6 Long
Distance Walks
Walking in the Isle Of Arran
Walking in the Lowther Hills
North to the Cape
The Border Country –
A Walker's Guide
Winter Climbs – Cairngorms
The Speyside Way
Winter Climbs – Ben Nevis &
Glencoe

The Isle of Skye, A Walker's Guide
The West Highland Way
Scotland's Far North
Walking the Munros Vol 1 –
  Southern, Central
Walking the Munros Vol 2 –
  Northern & Cairngorms
Scotland's Far West
Walking in the Cairngorms

IRELAND
The Mountains of Ireland
Irish Coastal Walks
The Irish Coast to Coast

INTERNATIONAL CYCLE GUIDES
The Way of St James – Le Puy to
  Santiago cyclist's guide
The Danube Cycle Way
Cycle Tours in Spain
Cycling the River Loire – The Way
  of St Martin

WALKING AND TREKKING
IN THE ALPS
Grand Tour of Monte Rosa Vol 1
Grand Tour of Monte Rosa Vol 2
Walking in the Alps (all Alpine
  areas)
100 Hut Walks in the Alps
Chamonix to Zermatt
Tour of Mont Blanc
Alpine Ski Mountaineering
  Vol 1 Western Alps
Alpine Ski Mountaineering
  Vol 2 Eastern Alps
Snowshoeing: Techniques and
  Routes in the Western Alps
Alpine Points of View

FRANCE, BELGIUM AND
LUXEMBOURG
The Tour of the Queyras
Rock Climbs in the Verdon
RLS (Robert Louis Stevenson) Trail
Walks in Volcano Country
French Rock
Walking the French Gorges
Rock Climbs Belgium &
  Luxembourg
Tour of the Oisans: GR54
Walking in the Tarentaise and
  Beaufortain Alps
The Brittany Coastal Path
Walking in the Haute Savoie
Walking in the Ardennes
Tour of the Vanoise
Walking in the Languedoc
GR20 Corsica – The High Level
  Route
The Ecrins National Park
Walking the French Alps: GR5
Walking in the Cevennes
Vanoise Ski Touring
Walking in Provence
Walking on Corsica
Mont Blanc Walks
Walking in the Cathar region
  of south west France
Walking in the Dordogne

PYRENEES AND FRANCE / SPAIN

Rock Climbs in the Pyrenees
Walks & Climbs in the Pyrenees
  The GR10 Trail: Through the
  French Pyrenees
The Way of St James –
  Le Puy to the Pyrenees
The Way of St James –
  Pyrenees-Santiago-Finisterre
Through the Spanish Pyrenees
  GR11
The Pyrenees – World's Mountain
  Range Guide
The Pyrenean Haute Route
Walking in Andorra

SPAIN AND PORTUGAL
Picos de Europa – Walks & Climbs
Andalusian Rock Climbs
The Mountains of Central Spain
Costa Blanca Rock
Walking in Mallorca
Rock Climbs in Majorca,
  Ibiza & Tenerife
Costa Blanca Walks Vol 1
Costa Blanca Walks Vol 2
Walking in Madeira
Via de la Plata (Seville To Santiago)
Walking in the Cordillera
  Cantabrica
Walking in the Canary Islands 1
  West
Walking in the Canary Islands 2
  East
Walking in the Sierra Nevada

SWITZERLAND
The Jura: Walking the High Route &
  Ski Traverses
Walking in Ticino, Switzerland
Central Switzerland –
  A Walker's Guide
The Bernese Alps
Walking in the Valais
Alpine Pass Route
Walks in the Engadine, Switzerland

GERMANY AND AUSTRIA
Klettersteig Scrambles in
  Northern Limestone Alps
King Ludwig Way
Walking in the Salzkammergut
Walking in the Black Forest
Walking in the Harz Mountains
Walking in the Bavarian Alps
Germany's Romantic Road
Mountain Walking in Austria
Walking the River Rhine Trail
Trekking in the Stubai Alps
Trekking in the Zillertal Alps

SCANDINAVIA
Walking In Norway
The Pilgrim Road to Nidaros
  (St Olav's Way)

EASTERN EUROPE
Trekking in the Caucausus
The High Tatras
The Mountains of Romania
Walking in Hungary

CROATIA AND SLOVENIA
Walks in the Julian Alps

Walking in Croatia

ITALY
Italian Rock
Walking in the Central Italian Alps
Central Apennines of Italy
Walking in Italy's Gran Paradiso
Long Distance Walks in Italy's Gran
  Paradiso
Walking in Sicily
Shorter Walks in the Dolomites
Treks in the Dolomites
Via Ferratas of the Italian
  Dolomites Vol 1
Via Ferratas of the Italian
  Dolomites Vol 2
Walking in the Dolomites
Walking in Tuscany
Trekking in the Apennines

OTHER MEDITERRANEAN
COUNTRIES
The Mountains of Greece
Climbs & Treks in the Ala Dag
  (Turkey)
The Mountains of Turkey
Treks & Climbs Wadi Rum, Jordan
Jordan – Walks, Treks, Caves etc.
Crete – The White Mountains
Walking in Palestine
Walking in Malta

AFRICA
Climbing in the Moroccan Anti-
  Atlas
Trekking in the Atlas Mountains
Kilimanjaro

NORTH AMERICA
The Grand Canyon &
  American South West
Walking in British Columbia
The John Muir Trail

SOUTH AMERICA
Aconcagua

HIMALAYAS – NEPAL, INDIA
Langtang, Gosainkund &
  Helambu: A Trekkers' Guide
Garhwal & Kumaon –
  A Trekkers' Guide
Kangchenjunga – A Trekkers' Guide
Manaslu – A Trekkers' Guide
Everest – A Trekkers' Guide
Annapurna – A Trekker's Guide
Bhutan – A Trekker's Guide
  DELAYED

AUSTRALIA AND NEW ZEALAND
Classic Tramps in New Zealand

TECHNIQUES AND EDUCATION
The Adventure Alternative
Rope Techniques
Snow & Ice Techniques
Mountain Weather
Beyond Adventure
The Hillwalker's Manual
The Book of the Bivvy
Outdoor Photography
The Hillwalker's Guide to
  Mountaineering
Map and Compass

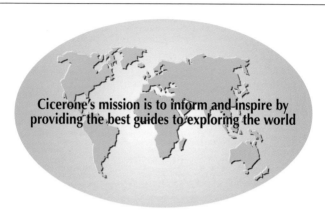

Cicerone's mission is to inform and inspire by
providing the best guides to exploring the world

Since its foundation over 30 years ago, Cicerone has specialised in publishing guidebooks and has built a reputation for quality and reliability. It now publishes nearly 300 guides to the major destinations for outdoor enthusiasts, including Europe, UK and the rest of the world.

Written by leading and committed specialists, Cicerone guides are recognised as the most authoritative. They are full of information, maps and illustrations so that the user can plan and complete a successful and safe trip or expedition – be it a long face climb, a walk over Lakeland fells, an alpine traverse, a Himalayan trek or a ramble in the countryside.

With a thorough introduction to assist planning, clear diagrams, maps and colour photographs to illustrate the terrain and route, and accurate and detailed text, Cicerone guides are designed for ease of use and access to the information.

If the facts on the ground change, or there is any aspect of a guide that you think we can improve, we are always delighted to hear from you.

Cicerone Press
2 Police Square Milnthorpe Cumbria LA7 7PY
Tel:01539 562 069   Fax:01539 563 417
e-mail:info@cicerone.co.uk   web:www.cicerone.co.uk

CICERONE